Tales of Darkness

Also available from *Continuum*:

Myth: Key Concepts in Religion, Robert Ellwood

Tales of Darkness

The Mythology of Evil

Robert Ellwood

Continuum
Continuum International Publishing Group
The Tower Building   80 Maiden Lane
11 York Road   Suite 704
London SE1 7NX   New York NY10038

www.continuumbooks.com

Copyright © Robert Ellwood 2009

All rights reserved. No part of this publication may be reproduced or transmitted in any form or by any means, electronic or mechanical, including photocopying, recording or any information storage, or retrieval system, without prior permission in writing from the publishers.

British Library Cataloguing-in-Publication Data
A catalogue record for this book is available from the British Library.

ISBN-13: HB: 978-0-8264-3714-3
        PB: 978-0-8264-3361-0

Library of Congress Cataloging-in-Publication Data
Ellwood, Robert S., 1933–
  Tales of darkness : The mythology of evil / Robert Ellwood.
    p. cm.
  Includes bibliographical references (p.   ) and index.
  ISBN 978-0-8264-3714-3—ISBN 978-0-8264-3661-0
  1. Good and evil. 2. Mythology. 3. Myth. I. Title.

BJ406.E45 2009
170—dc22
            2009016174

Typeset by RefineCatch Limited, Bungay, Suffolk

Contents

Introduction: *The Abomination of Desolation: Introducing Evil and Myth*   1

Part I   Evil Is Abroad   11

1. Defilement   13
2. Evil People   20
3. Space Invaders   29
4. The Way Things Are   37
5. Couldn't It Have Happened Differently?   46
6. Trickster's Gameplan   53
7. Traumatic Initiations   62
8. The Hero's Dragon   71
9. Evil under Analysis   82

Part II   The Road Back: Curing Evil   93

10. Laughter and Wisdom   95
11. Through Death to Life   99

12	The Hero Victorious	109
13	The Meaning of War	119
14	The End of Days	132
15	Summing Up	141
Bibliography		147
Notes		149
Index		161

Introduction

The Abomination of Desolation: Introducing Evil and Myth

Night, Ice and Pride

The great ship *Titanic* sank on the night of 14–15 April 1912, after collision with an iceberg on her maiden voyage. As much as any event in the twentieth or twenty-first centuries, that night to remember has become a myth in its own right: a tale of darkness which, told over and over, seems to bear significance beyond itself to offer a general view of human nature, of the meaning of human experience in its own time and ours, and even of the dynamics of the cosmos itself.

The *Titanic* story is familiar. It was about midnight. Out on the death-cold North Atlantic floated a human-made centre of light and jovial life, tiny compared to the vastness of the alien sea. Yet it was a ship of dreams. On the part of those at the top when Britain ruled the waves and America seemed the land of the future, theirs was an age of egregious opulence, and not seldom arrogance; self-assuredness and fantasies of self-importance were on display amid the glittering elegance of First Class dining rooms and club rooms. People in other ranks held their own compelling reveries at the same time, set future rather than now; the hopeful reveries of immigrants down below were full of expectations for their soon-to-begin new life in a new world.

For the world of 1912 was a world of belief in progress, in the amenities of human life improving year by year through science and engineering. No less powerful was belief that society was getting better and better at a comparable pace through improved education, expanding democracy and rising standards of living for workers as well as the wealthy.

Titanic seemed to be a visionary vessel bearing the weight of that cargo. She was the most advanced ship afloat, reportedly unsinkable. Her sophisticated salons echoed the talk of civilization at its height, and even Third Class was said to eat and sleep better than the dismal steerage quarters of only a few decades earlier. But nature had something else in mind than the triumphal inaugural sailing from Southampton to New York. In the words of Thomas Hardy's famous 1912 poem about that night, 'The Convergence of the Twain':

> Well: while was fashioning
> This creature of cleaving wing,
> The Immanent Will that stirs and urges everything
>
> Prepared a sinister mate
> For her – so gaily great –
> A Shape of Ice, for the time fat and dissociate,
>
> And as the smart ship grew
> In statue, grace, and hue
> In shadowy silent distance grew the Iceberg too
>
> Alien they seemed to be;
> No mortal eye could see
> The intimate welding of their later history . . .

We know what happened: the night was dark and moonless over the North Atlantic, the waters lay calm as a millpond, the crow's-nest binoculars were missing: all conditions that made the ship's icy nemesis almost impossible for lookouts to see. Suddenly the jarring encounter ripped a great gash along the vessel's side, then followed slow sinking and panicked evacuation, which made dreadfully clear that far fewer lifeboats were provided than needed. Survivors were disproportionately women and children from First Class. Of the 2,224 persons aboard, 1,513, well over half, perished in the near-freezing waters.

Evil had intruded, if by evil we mean that which causes suffering, which intrudes on what we think ought to be the rightful course of events, and maims or cuts short any life well before it has fulfilled its natural cycle. All too soon, the horrors of 1914, of a world at war, were to shatter the illusions of a more innocent day far more profoundly. But back to April, 1912. What happened in the darkness of that night was the stuff of myth, and soon enough it was myth, culminating in James Cameron's famous 1997 movie, *Titanic*.

What was the cause of that particular evil? Twofold, nature and human thoughts, words, and deed. The iceberg, slowly forming of itself from glaciers in distant Greenland even as the great ship was being built in the yards of Belfast, was certainly one source, and raises the eternal question, why does nature often seem hostile to humankind? But other questions of meaning come to mind as well: why the arrogance of those who considered the ship unsinkable, the heedlessness of not providing enough lifeboats, the pride of kind which so divided the passengers into classes hardly aware of one another as real people? All these issues we will find explored over and over in myth.

The movie *Titanic* added another theme to cosmic and general human sources of evil – the hero myth, with its implication that one way to understand evil is the mythic way, that is, through the medium of story. This film frames evil, both natural and human, as adversary a hero must overcome. A story is very different from a philosophical proposition. For story, evil cannot just be privation of good, or a lower stage of evolution, or such conflict as must arise in a universe of many parts jostling for pride of place. Story calls for a protagonist, and an obstacle that individual must conquer. Often the obstacle is personified: a dragon or other monster, a human antagonist of malignant character.

In the picture, the hero is a young woman, Rose, who must descend into the depths of the sinking ship to rescue her love, Jack, chained far below by the 'bad guy'. The adversary is not only that sinister individual, but the ship itself, which becomes like a monster of the deep, groaning as the metal twists, lights flashing on and off like baleful eyes as water reaches the power sources, while Rose continues her desperate quest. When she is finally victorious, we sense that in myth evil is not only a quirk of nature, or the fruit of human folly, but also can even exist for the sake of the hero, to perfect his or her strength through the battle that must be fought and the adversary that must be overcome. Evil exists, so to speak, not only as part of the story, but for the sake of the story. To understand this, we must understand myth as meaning in story form.

Which Comes First?

In a book on the mythology of evil, which comes first: a definition of myth, or of evil? Both go together, and one cannot be understood without the other. In mythological perspective, evil becomes part of a narrative. As we have seen, wickedness is not a philosophical abstraction. It tells a story, and the tale must possess the basic characteristics of story.

As any writer knows, a story needs a plot, and the plot requires some problem or hindrance to be overcome. The barrier can be defined mythically as evil. But any good writer, and any good mythmaker, must have also taken to heart the writing school dictum: Show, don't tell. The obstacle must be presented in guise of an enemy or force seen or felt; that is what makes a *myth* of evil, in contrast to a metaphysical or theological abstraction endeavouring to explain it. Then, the terror seen and felt can best be made palpable by putting it at the heart of a story: the iron gate to be overleaped, the cunning foe to be outsmarted, the dark knight to be bested in fair combat.

A myth or story of evil will not answer all questions that could arise, for behind every story a possible backstory always lurks. We can say that God was Creator of heaven and earth, but one can then ask, as children often do, where did God come from? Where was evil before it oozed its way into our once happy fields? What happened before to make ours the kind of world in which a given story could take place?

But first and final questions are not insurmountable problems in relation to evil, for evil in the end is always the inexplicable. It is that which ought not to be, yet is – in the language of scripture, 'The abomination of desolation ... standing where it ought not' (Mark 13: 14).

So much in the glorious universe around us suggests a smooth, harmonious system. The stars in their courses, the circling planets, the turn of the seasons, even the natural order built into biology – birth, childhood, maturity, aging and death – point towards a profound yet rational plan, almost mathematical in its precision, like a beautiful ship sailing on its maiden voyage across a serene sea.

Then something else breaks in, shattering the mosaic of balanced colours, drowning out the glorious symphony in discordant notes, like clash of ice and metal. For all we know, whole world-systems teeming with life-forms may be swallowed up suddenly and mercilessly every day by supernova or black holes. Here on planet earth, thousand perish or suffer excruciating agony regularly, from fire, flood and famine. Few creatures born into this world, in fact, complete the full life-cycle programmed into their genetic inheritance. These include not only those fish of whose innumerable spawn only a few survive to adulthood, or those countless beasts whose lives we cut short for our own purposes, but also those human beings who die young of war or disease, or who fall far short of all they could be out of poverty and exploitation.

Tracks in the Dark

These are the tracks of that other, and explaining his sordid career has tested the wit of the most brilliant philosophers. Not a few otherwise scintillating systems of thought have lost lustre as they tried to explain why, in a world of so many dimensions of wonder and harmony, and many would say created by God both all-powerful and all-good, the Abomination nonetheless stands, his force hardly softened after innumerable cycles of sentient life. Or, giving up metaphysical or theological ventures, they have fallen into the sort of naturalism that leaves the matter in the hands of impersonal evolutionary forces, in which at best it is the survival of the species that matters. Individual pain can only be interpreted in proximate, perhaps medical, ways, and then minimized as far as possible. But one may ask whether philosophy can give the ultimate answers in language that is not simply tautology, such as saying that by definition nothing and no one created God because the deity dwells in aseity, self-existence.

In the same way, in myth and story we can tell how particular manifestations of evil appeared, perhaps all the way back to war in heaven before the earth was formed, and – this myth is good at – we can delineate all the virtues and strategies needed to combat evil. So myth, like all religion 'makes the universe humanly significant', in the words of Peter Berger.[1] Myth and religion, unlike science, present no cosmos of blind forces and inert matter spinning galaxies, stars and solar systems out of a Big Bang, but one of minds and feelings which, though larger in scale than ours, are nonetheless kin to the human.

C. S. Lewis, in one of the Narnia stories, *The Voyage of the Dawn Treader*, takes the characters to a remote island where they meet the conscious spirit of a star. One of the visitors, the sceptical Eustace, says, 'In our world a star is a huge ball of flaming gas.' The star responds, 'Even in your world, my son, that is not what a star is but only what it is made of.'[2]

In the same way, someone might say that a human being is salt water plus various carbon-based compounds. We might well respond, 'That's what a human being is made of, but not what a human being is.'

So it could be that nature only appears to be mostly inert matter; inwardly it may also be animated by gods and spirits humanly significant, and not alien to us as humans. Not surprisingly, then, the gods are capable of what to us appears evil, as well as good, and we are more than capable of getting caught up in their rights and wrongs.

Plumed Serpent and Blood Moon

Take a Maya myth, which tells us that the gods Hurricane and Plumed Serpent made several mistakes in creating humans. First they made them too soft and they fell to pieces; then too wooden and no more able to remember anything than a piece of furniture. Finally, attempting to destroy these futile attempts, the creators sent storm and flood so excessively terrible it upset the natural order, placing speaking animals in the homes of people.

When the waters finally settled, a monstrous bird had set himself over the dismal remains: 'This was when there was just a trace of early dawn on the face of the earth, there was no sun. But there was one who magnified himself; Seven Macaw is his name.'[3] The arrogant avian was finally defeated by the hero gods Hunapuh and Xbalanque, sons of a god and an underworld maiden named Blood Moon. After many other adventures these two had prepared the earth for the finally-successful human creations of Hurricane and Plumed Serpent.

We humans can relate to such a story, for we too have often proved inept at what we have tried to do, and have suffered from unintended consequences. For the great virtue of myth, as it presents meaning in the form of story, is that it makes possible an immediate human connection. As one cannot emphasize too often, our lives are stories, not philosophical or scientific abstractions.

A myth alien to one's own time and culture, like this one, can appear too bizarre, at least without much interpretation, to be directly relevant. But if the tale leaves a place where we can fit in, it does something no abstraction however profound can do, it provides a larger story into which our own can slip, thereby giving ours larger meaning, and offering us great roles which we can try to let our lives reflect.

What Is Myth?

Myth has several meanings today. For the 'person on the street', and in much of journalism, it simply means a story that is not true: 'That's just a myth.' Obviously, that sense is not adequate for those who, like the present writer, feel the term may be used respectfully in relation to a certain kind of story found in religious and cultural lore – though, because of the vernacular meaning, one remains open to any suggestion of a better word.

The myth kind of story presents a society's basic worldview and values in narrative form. The story not only lays out the geography of the narrator's earth, and as well the heavens and the underworlds, but also suggests responses to its realities. Do we respond with laughter or tears? With a sense of cosmic absurdity or with malice? Acceptance, or the pose of the hero setting out to battle and slay a dragon personifying evil? Myths can be found articulating all these responses and more. The point is, if it is myth, that response is given in the form of story.

For myth is, in the sense of Paul Ricoeur, a species of symbol. It is language which, unlike allegory, has multiple levels of meaning that point beyond itself to more and more universal perspectives on human experience and the sacred. Myth is symbol in narrative form.[4] The story of Adam and Eve not only offers an explanation of evil, but points to exile as an ultimate metaphor for the human situation. The function of myth, then, is to universalize the human condition, to show the tension between the ideal and the real, to reveal but not allegorize that condition – in the same way as does any great literature, which does not present a mere allegory of life, but tells a human tale so well we may say, 'That story helped me understand who I am, and what the world is really like.'

Among those who take myth seriously, two schools obtain. One, perhaps especially classicists, tends to restrict the term to stories about gods and heroes with sources in preliterate, oral culture, and which provide models for the values and behaviour of the society: for its social and political organization, and the origin of its major rites and landmarks. Thus the *Theogony* and *Works and Days* of Hesiod tell the origin of the Olympian gods whose worship dominated Greek civic life, and in his story of Pandora he explained the origin of evil – in a woman's curiosity. The other school emphasizes the continuing life and importance of myth in our world. It delights in considering such recent works in the mythic mode as J. R. R. Tolkien's *The Lord of the Rings*, or such cinematic epics as *Star Wars* or the already-mentioned *Titanic* to be real myths, all the more relevant because of their contemporary provenance, however fantasy-land their setting.

Even in the case of classical mythology, is it really the doubtless fragmentary and inconsistent local, oral stories gathered up by such bards as Homer in Greece or the Anglo-Saxon poet of *Beowulf* that are the myth, or is it the product of those master wordsmiths, who gave us the works read by countless schoolboys and girls, which have inspired innumerable dramas and now films, which have become the sacred lore of nations and religions? The scholar A. H. Krappe went so far as to say that myth is essentially the work of epic poets, usually read as fiction unless it happens to become incorporated into the sacred texts of a religion.[5] One can go round and round in arguments like this; we can only say that without the poets and scribes we would hardly know these great epics, much less think of them as world-significant myths. Both sides are obviously significant. Whatever the literary worth of the finished mythical product, it also offers us as vital a glimpse as we have into the thought-world of preliterate human: how they perceived the world, how they remembered and conveyed essential information, how they inculcated values for upcoming generations, why for them story was far more than just entertainment.

The World of Oral Culture

So then, do really significant difference lie between ways of understanding and assimilating, even between ways of thinking, in oral and literate cultures? A study by Aleksandr R. Luria, a Soviet psychologist, based on 1930s interviews with illiterate and newly literate peasants in Uzbekistan and Kyrgyzstan found that between the two groups marked differences did exist.[6] Illiterates thought in terms of stories, while literates could deal in abstract categories. For example, illiterates were shown a picture containing a hammer, a saw, an axe and a log, and were asked to name the three that were similar.

The non-readers said they were all useful. If forced to decide, they would leave out the hammer, saying it would never cut wood like saw or axe. Clearly, they were not thinking in terms of generic categories – tools versus logs – but in terms of how one might tell a story about these objects, a story about doing something like cutting wood. When told that some viewers had grouped the three tools together, excluding the log, they laughed, saying 'That person must have enough firewood already.'

When shown a picture of three adults and a child and asked which one of those didn't fit, they refused to exclude the child, saying he needed them and the adults needed the child to run errands. Again, the picture immediately becomes not a puzzle but a story – thinking by means of story-telling. Getting this, we know where myths came from as we trace them back far before the invention of writing into the mists of prehistory.

For non-literate oral culture, then, understanding immediately becomes an exercise in story rather than abstract logic. Orals store their thoughts in stories. There is more: as another student of orality and reading, Walter J. Ong, has pointed out, to be memorable, and so remembered, a story needs protagonists and opponents, us and them. It calls for conflict, and violent and passionate events, to summon up the 'juices' that energize good memorization – the tale must become *myth*, not mere chronicle.[7] In that mythic tale evil, as enemy or obstacle, must be there to be overcome.

However, while myth may be born in oral culture, it does not die with the coming of letters. Both read and recited, the Iliad and Odyssey of Homer, and the Aeniad of Virgil, were officially-sanctioned sacred vessels containing perspective values underlying the Greco-Roman world. Other vessels obtained as well. Not a few officers of the Roman legions were partisans of the myth and worship of Mithras, and other Romans, particularly perhaps women, favoured the Egyptian goddess Isis, the divine mother of a thousand names. Some such stories may have been written, but many others, important to particular groups, were probably only transmitted orally, as if the age of writing had never come.

Today, myths live in many media: print, radio, television, cinema and tales told in the office, the school playground, or the living room. Modern myth may take the form of 'urban legends', which seemingly come from nowhere, or perchance happened to the proverbial 'friend of a friend'. But they are told and retold, no doubt because they symbolize some diffuse modern hope or dread.

In the nineteenth and early twentieth centuries, the ancient British mythology associated with King Arthur and Camelot had an impressive vogue,[8] as did the ancient German mythology presented through the operas of Richard Wagner in Wilhelmine Germany, or the ancient Shinto myths of imperial ancestry revived in modern Japan. All had a significant role in emergent national consciousness. In the late twentieth and early twenty-first centuries, interestingly, the mythology shaping popular consciousness has tended to be less nationalistic than set in fantasy or futuristic worlds: C. S. Lewis' Narnia stories, the TV and movie epics *Star Trek* and *Star Wars*. We will return to these and other modern myths.

Part I

Evil Is Abroad

Chapter 1

Defilement

The Ground Accursed

In some myths of evil, setting is the real antagonist. Earth and sky themselves bespeak a pervasive presence of evil: call it defilement, spiritual pollution, accursed land. In tales of fear, or evoking fright, from grim fairy tales like many of those of the Brothers Grimm to horror movies, the real enemy is nothing so much as fear itself, that primal dread which paralyses thought . . . and which often seems really to stem from the setting, as it were the soil itself underlying the story.

Take for example these lines from the prophet Amos, in the Hebrew scriptures: the devastation of the land seems far more vivid even than the Lord who sent it:

> I blasted you with black blight and red;
> I laid waste your gardens and vineyards;
> the locust devoured your fig-trees and your olives;
> yet you did not come back to me.
> This is the very word of the Lord.
> I sent plague upon you like the plagues of Egypt;
> I killed with the sword
> your young men and your troops of horses.
> I made your camps stink in your nostrils;
> yet you did not come back to me.
> This is the very word of the Lord. [Amos 4: 9–10; The New English Bible]

Moving west to England, consider the wasteland in the story of the Holy Grail. One version tells that the land became desolate in this way.

The castle was called Carbonek; the kingdom Listinois; its ruler was the worthy King Pellam, guardian of the greatest relics in Christendom, the Holy Grail and Holy Lance, the cup from which Christ had drunk at the Last Supper, and the spear which had pierced his side on the Cross.

But the king's brother, Garlon, a troublemaker who ravaged the surrounding lands, also made this high keep his home base. A certain one of King Arthur's knights, Balin, quick-tempered and full of outrage at Garlon, closed on him at Carbonek, and there put the scoundrel to death. Pellam, not fully realizing who this strange bringer of violence to his house was, drew weapons against Balin, and in the scuffle the latter lost his sword. Panicking, the knight of Arthur ran through the palace, dashing from room to room:

> And at the last he entered into a chamber that was marvellously well dight and richly . . . and there[in] stood a table of clean gold and four pillars of silver that bare up the table, and upon the table stood a marvellous spear strangely wrought . . .[9]

Balin may have paused for a moment struck with the wonder of this mystical place, but only for a moment. King Pellam quickly charged in, sword drawn, determined to confront the intruder. Responding like a trapped animal, Balin grabbed the spear, which of course was none other than the Holy Lance, and thrust it into the King's groin: this was called the Dolorous Stroke.

The knight felt a burning sensation, and then all went dark. After he recovered the next morning, as he rode back through his land:

> [H]e found trees down and grain destroyed and all things laid waste, as if lightning had struck in each place, and unquestionably it had struck in many places, though not everywhere. He found half the people in the villages dead, both bourgeois and knights, and he found laborers dead in the fields. What can I tell you? He found the kingdom of Listinois so totally destroyed that it was later called by everyone the Kingdom of Waste Land and the Kingdom of Strange Land, because everywhere the land had become so strange and wasted.[10]

Clearly, the overwhelming reality at this point is the desolation of field and forest. This particular devastation seems somehow strange, as it were uncanny, its foulness the product of no mere act of nature. The reversal of the defilement would be the task of the grandest quest of all those undertaken by King Arthur's Knights of the Table Round, the quest for the Holy Grail. For only by finding again Carbonek and its priceless treasure, now half hidden from this defiled world, and saying words which rightly honoured it, could that kingdom again bloom. The tension between defilement and human hope explored in the Grail story underlies many a myth.

Eden and Mecca

In Islam, tradition relates that earth was Eden, a paradise, before the sin and the expulsion of Adam and Eve. But after their fall the fair land became a polluted realm of delusion. With the coming of the Prophet, however, the world could be divided between Dar al-Islam, the House of Submission to Allah, and Dar al-Harb, the House of Conflict. The House of Islam is crucially important in this post-Edenic age, because now humans require civilization to maintain order and obtain food and other necessities; in our need Islam lays out the right, divinely-sanctioned way to order society.

At the heart of Islam stands the prayer and pilgrimage centre of Mecca, 'Mecca, the Blessed', which in many ways is a symbolic outpost of Eden yet remaining on earth. In particular, prayers directed towards the holy city, while still holding to the order of civilization, suggests the union of Eden and now. Brannon Wheeler writes, 'Facing Mecca during the group prayer, people direct their attention towards Mecca and its symbolism as a substitute for the lost Eden, while standing in rows and thus delineating their social and economic standing on the society of the postfall world.'[11] By the same token, the Hajj or pilgrimage, as pilgrims approach the sacred centre in unsewn garb, abstaining from sex and violence, and circumambulate the Ka'bah, said to be the place of earth closest to heaven, is a symbolic return to the primal purity of Eden.

In this mytho-religious worldview, then, relative degrees of purity and pollution are distributed unevenly through both time and, as a remnant of times past, geographical space: Eden is partially perpetuated in Mecca. The reversal of the equivalent of the dolorous stroke is a process continuing until the end of this age of the world; in a real sense it must be done by each believer for him- or herself.

The Outcast's Touch

In some myths of evil, the pollution may be human: those persons can be met whose very presence sullies, and from whose touch we shrink, and likewise certain animals are impure. We will look later at the case of witches, lepers, outcasts, those possessed by unclean spirits, and others in this unhappy category. In all cases, pollution has a cause, for the world was not created impure, nor was an individual born unblessed – or his or her ancestors, if it is the hereditary impurity of an unclean group or caste that is invoked. A myth can generally be found to explain how this place or face became besmirched, like the story of how the murderer of Abel acquired the mark of Cain – which saved the victim's brother from being killed in turn, but which sent him wandering east of Eden and away from God. (Gen. 4: 15)

But in the stories of which we are now thinking, defilement, and the vague but powerful feelings to which it gives rise, seem the central reality, the cause almost an afterthought. As Paul Ricoeur wrote, 'Defilement itself is scarcely a representation, and what representation there is is immersed in a specific sort of fear that blocks reflection. With defilement we enter into the reign of Terror.'[12] This same author views this general sense of stain, of contamination, of sin and dread of retribution, so potent that further precise analysis is barred. The origin of evil cannot be fully understood by humans, yet in turn knowing evil makes us spiritually human: 'That is why the primitive dread deserves to be interrogated as our oldest memory.'[13]

Shudderings of Horror

Pollution can be recent, yet create anguish comparable to original sin. A few lines from Jane Austen's novel *Mansfield Park*, describing how Fanny felt on learning that her cousin Maria, after only six months of marriage, had run off with another man, tells the inner atmosphere of dark, shapeless dread, anxiety, shame and guilt (even though it was not her guilt personally) called up by such a transgression in the basic order of the world she knew.

> The horror of a mind like Fanny's, as it received the conviction of such guilt, and began to take in some part of the misery that must ensue, can hardly be described. At first, it was a sort of stupefication; but every moment was quickening her perception

of the horrible evil ... There was no possibility of rest. The evening passed, without a pause of misery, the night was totally sleepless. She passed only from feelings of sickness to shudderings of horror; and from hot fits to cold.[14]

In Euripides' great drama *Orestes*, the hero of that name is polluted by his own commission of matricide, the murder of his mother, Clytemnestra, and her lover, Aegisthus, in revenge for her murder of his father Agamemnon upon the commander's return from the Trojan war, and for her adultery. Orestes believed he was ordered by the oracle at Delphi to commit this deed. Here his sister and co-conspirator, Elektra, describes the state of pollution to which this crime, however justified, reduced the perpetrator. Not only was there the pollution itself, but he was also pursued by the Erinyes (Furies), until Athena finally calmed them and changed them into the Eumenides (Kindly Ones) as she forgave Orestes. Here are the words of Elektra describing her brother's state:

> After this my poor Orestes fell sick to a cruel wasting disease; upon his couch he lies prostrated, and it is his mother's blood that goads him into frenzied fits; this I say, from dread of naming those goddesses, whose terrors are chasing him before them, even the Eumenides. 'Tis now the sixth day since the body of his murdered mother was committed to the cleansing fire; since then no food has passed his lips, nor hath he washed his skin; but wrapped in his cloak he weeps in his lucid moments, whenever the fever leaves him; other whiles he bounds headlong from his couch, as a colt when it is loosed from the yoke.[15]

Or consider the contest of Apollo with Python, representing respectively purity and pollution. Python was an earth-monster originally sent by Hera, wife of Zeus, to torment Leto, mother of Apollo, in revenge for her spouse's adulterous affair with her, one of many on the part of that promiscuous deity, and one of many such acts of retribution on the part of the god's incensed mate.

Apollo in turn shot Python as he was guarding the oracle-shrine of Delphi, thus purifying the holy place and making that sacred site his own. It was regarded as the geographical centre of the world, and innumerable suppliants, including kings and statesmen, came to Delphi for the often-enigmatic words spoken in trance by the pythia, the mediumistic woman believed to be the voice of Apollo himself. The temple thus represented the organized world, and the deity Apollo – often contrasted with Dionysus, god of drink and excess – represented beauty and restraint, as over against chaos and the pollution it engenders. It was Apollo who also finally purified Orestes from the pollution of having killed his mother for her adultery.

Always Winter, Never Christmas

Turning to modern tales in the mythic mode, consider *The Lion, the Witch and the Wardrobe*, the first of C. S. Lewis' beloved Narnia series of children's tales. Here Lucy describes the usurper ruling in Narnia:

> She isn't a real queen at all ... she's a horrible witch, the White Witch. Every one – all the wood people – hate her. She has made an enchantment over the whole country so that it is always winter here and never Christmas.[16]

Another modern mythopoeic writer, J. R. R. Tolkien, in the third book of his great fantasy *The Lord of the Rings*, well evokes how Frodo and Sam bore the Ring into the land of Mordor, 'Where the shadows lie.' It was the Dark Lord's greatest weapon, formless fear and dread, that most lay upon them:

> For the hobbits each day, each mile, was more bitter than the one before, as their strength lessened and the land became more evil. They met no enemies by day. At times by night, as they cowered or drowsed uneasily in some hiding beside the road, they heard cries and the noise of many feet or the swift passing of some cruelly ridden steed. But far worse than all such perils was the ever-approaching threat that beat upon them as they went: the dreadful menace of the Power that waited, brooding in deep thought and sleepless malice behind the dark veil about its Throne. Nearer and nearer it drew, looming blacker, like the oncoming of wall of night at the last end of the world.[17]

Many powerful writers have evoked the particular feeling of dread, wrong, the breakdown of human order and of something that should not be yet is, amidst the horror that is war, ancient or modern. Not a few warriors, like Henry Fleming in Stephen Crane's great novel of the American Civil War, *The Red Badge of Courage*, have found that they first went out to battle full of chivalrous idealism, wishing to fight an honourable war for a righteous cause. But soon enough the day came when the glory faded, and all that remained was a fierce loyalty to one's fellow-soldiers, together with a nervous fear in which one does not really sleep, watches all things warily, shoots at anything unknown that moves.

There are causes for war, of course, both official and unofficial, but for those in the midst of it the great reality is simply the abomination within which one finds oneself. In *The Red Badge of Courage*, Crane called up with especial vividness the sheer confusion amid horror of the field of battle itself; this chaos is, in its own time, the great fact of the soldier's life; and over that chaos, in the line of Poe, 'Death looks gigantically down.'[18] Crane wrote:

> There was a consciousness always of the presence of his comrades about him. He felt the subtle battle brotherhood more potent even than the cause for which they were fighting. It was a mysterious fraternity born of the smoke and danger of death . . .
> Presently he began to feel the effects of the war atmosphere – a blistering sweat, a sensation that his eyeballs were about to crack like hot stones. A burning rage filled his ears . . .
> Buried in the smoke of many rifles his anger was directed not so much against the men who he knew were rushing toward him as against the swirling battle phantoms which were choking him, snuffing their smoke robes down his parched throat. He fought frantically for respite for his senses, for air, as a babe being smothered attacks the deadly blankets.[19]

In sum, then, we can begin the pursuit of the mythology of evil with the powerful sense of pollution, of defilement, that early humans – and many later people – felt in certain places, in certain other persons, after certain things had been done, no doubt often within themselves. It was necessary to ascribe a cause to this effect, since the proper state of the universe must be order and cleanliness. Usually a cause is eventually found, though it may be messaged in a shaman's trance or by divination. A taboo had been broken, an unjust death had been perpetrated, a usurper sat on the throne. Yet that defilement – that plague, that blight on the land, that smoke of battle – spoke of its own of something wrong even before the cause was found; here is certainly one source of awareness that there is evil in the world, the abomination of desolation standing where it ought not.

Chapter 2

Evil People

Witches in Africa

Here is a story of witchcraft from the Congo region of Africa. In that troubled land, serious misfortunes and unexpected deaths are commonly attributed to witches. Witches (often male*) assemble from time to time to eat human flesh; each diner is expected in turn to bring a corpse to the grisly banquet. The victims are often unwilling relatives or neighbours. The story is told of a young woman named Malemba who went to visit her lover. He – unbeknownst to her – was such a witch. He was not at home, so she went quietly into his hut at twilight, so she would not be seen by others, and waited in a corner for him to return.

When the witch/lover re-entered his house, he did not see Malemba in her hiding place. Apparently a bit hungry, he proceeded to take down a basket of food, evidently provided by others of his coven. The girl was horrified to see him pull a human finger out of it, and proceed to eat the digit with relish. She was then even more terrified when she heard him, muttering to himself, abuse his brother witches for leaving him only this skinny, bony part of the luscious cadaver. He said to himself they would get no better when he killed his promised victim, Malemba.

The man then lit a torch, and saw Malemba there. Making an excuse, he left – she was sure her lover was now ready to bring in the other witches and begin the feast. She ran in terror back to her own village. But six witches, now collected, set out after her in the pursuit of dinner. They used a magical pointing-stick which, twisting around as with a life of its own, quickly pointed right at the young girl to direct them down her path.

Sprinting desperately just ahead of the malicious band, she got to her mother's garden barely in time to hide under a pile of brush. But all seemed lost when the witches, with the help of the sorcerer's stick, soon located her refuge. However, she was saved for a day when an antelope ran nearby, throwing them off long enough to allow her to enter her parents' house. Sorrowful and near death from her horrible adventure, she lay abed all the day, refusing to eat. That evening the sinister six returned, ostensibly on a mere visit; the sight of them so shocked Malemba that she then died.

The girl's outraged parents saw to it that the heartless intruders were punished. They were brought before the tribal council, and condemned to drink a poison which was said to be deathly to the guilty but harmless to the innocent. All died.[20]

This story does not tell why the six men were witches. But it does make clear that they were outside the proper structures of society, dwelling literally or figuratively in a twilight world, neither one way nor another. But they could be convicted by legitimate authority, and eliminated from the daytime social order.

In some parts of Africa, witches can split themselves into two: half can be peacefully asleep, while another, invisible half is out doing deeds of evil. Often the witches' world is upside down: the malefactors go out at night, when respectable people are at home; they may even walk with their legs upside down. Naked, they may eat human flesh, or have orgies with animals; all outside, opposite to, the proper human behaviour of a well-ordered society.[21]

One source of evil in myth, then, is not only polluted land, but polluted people; they are known, even apart from their deed, by the way they do not fit into, and stand apart from, the world of order. They are *other*, strange and ominous, and moreover possess strange frightening powers.

Baba Yaga and Her Kind

Consider also the story of Baba Yaga, the Russian cannibalistic ogress who kidnaps children, then cooks and eats them. She lives deep in the woods in a windowless house standing on chicken legs, which make the house able to walk around on its own. Baba Yaga also is able to rise out through the chimney and fly through the air on a mortar. Occasionally she is helpful, or at least ambivalent, but always dangerous to approach.[22] Baba may have originally been a patron goddess of women, a divine status perhaps reflected in accounts she has three horses representing Day, Sun and Night, though in Christian times she was degraded to witch.

Why did she, and other such, become witches? In old Russia, peasants made a difference between two kinds of witches, 'natural' witches who were 'born' to that evil work, and those who willingly chose the identity. 'Born' witches had inherited their power, or were given it directly by the devil in his own way. It could also happen that a person might unintentionally acquire witch-powers by carelessly touching or receiving an object imbued with that dark energy from a dying servant of Satan. They could still find salvation through repentance and special church rituals.

'Willing' sorcerers, thought to be more powerful, had of their own choice made a pact with the devil (typically at a crossroad or in a bathhouse). They had thrown away the cross around their necks, trampled on an icon face down, and disavowed allegiance to God, father and mother, and sometimes earth, sun and moon. Thus renouncing all that is good, they sold their souls to the evil one; he had then appeared in some horrendous guise to greet his new servant, now empowered to wield the black forces known to wizardry.

It may be added that the pact was not always successfully completed; folklore says that sometimes an apprentice became so terrified at the visible appearance of Satan or his high representative that he or she ran away, often to his death.[23]

Witch Hunts Then

In considering witchcraft as a source of evil, we must give regard not only to the evil allegedly done by witches themselves, but also to evil resulting from fear of witches by supposedly good people. Think of the great witch hunts of Europe approximately 1450–1700, together with the famous witch hysteria in Salem, Massachusetts, in 1692. Some estimates of the number of witch hunt victims have been exaggerated; current scholarly opinion puts the numbers at around 110,000 trials and 60,000 executions.[24] In any case, it was certainly a horrible event for those persecuted as witches, the majority (though not all) women. Beyond those figures, the 'scare' created an atmosphere of fear which surely afflicted many not actually brought to trial.

Suspects, when not just objects of someone's personal vendetta, were likely to be persons (as in Africa) deemed a bit unusual, perhaps wiser in the lore of nature than was normal, perhaps exhibiting such signs as an animal 'familiar', the evil eye, or an obscure bodily mark identified as the 'devil's teat'. They might then be hideously tortured, perhaps until (willing to say anything to stop the torture) they confessed to the whole array of current witchcraft fantasies: signing a pact with the devil, riding on a broomstick to the 'witches' sabbath', dancing and perhaps copulating with Satan.

What is it that characterizes the witchcraft of these narratives? Careful scholarship has brought out several significant features of the witch craze. More often than not, witch trials that ended in conviction and execution were in rural areas. They tended to occur most in areas lacking strong central government, such as much-divided Germany during the Thirty Years' War, or in border areas between nations, cultures, and – in those days of bitter religious conflict – between Catholic and Protestant districts.

As in the case of African witchcraft, then, suspicion focused on marginal persons, marginal situations, times of change – in other words people, places, times that did not fit into an orderly scheme. The great witch-fear occurred in a time when Europe, religiously divided and wrenching itself painfully into the modern world, experienced deep anxiety about what was happening and what the future forebode. Accusations of witchcraft, and even belief in it, were far less prevalent in the preceding Middle Ages.

'Satanic Panic' Now

Coming still closer to our own time, consider the 'Satanic panic' of the years around the 1980s which swept through the United States, Britain and other English-speaking countries. Numerous articles appeared in the popular media presenting accounts of 'ritual abuse' replete with Satanic symbols, including the sacrifice of babies. Often this was alleged to take place at preschools and day-care centres, based on the accounts of children who reportedly told counsellors and police officers of strange 'games' or 'plays' in which they were expected to engage. These often were said to involve sodomy, 'devil' masks and robes, animal or human body parts, and even the 'sacrifice' of babies.

The most notorious case was the 1984–1990 trial involving the McMartin preschool in a suburb of Los Angeles, which ended up being the most expensive court case in California history. Despite extensive colourful testimony from children and parents, no 'hard' evidence of crime was ever found, no bodies or definitely satanic artefacts, and in the end the defendant teachers and proprietors of the school were released after two successive juries had deadlocked. But the McMartin teachers, and other even less fortunate individuals who were convicted and imprisoned in these bizarre cases, found their schools, careers, and lives ruined nonetheless.[25]

It is now almost universally believed that the Satanic panic was spurious, despite its promotion by certain wings of resurgent evangelical Christianity. Perhaps it too reflected anxious and changing times. This was in fact the first generation of families in which both husband and wife typically went out to work, perforce leaving young children in day-care centres and preschools. Deep concerns as to whether this was right, and what kind of care their priceless young ones would actually have, may have been projected into satanic fantasies. One can only speculate.

The Meaning of Witchcraft

The anthropologist Mary Douglas, a specialist in Africa, in works like *Natural Symbols* and *Purity and Danger*, has emphasized that a culture's ultimate concern regarding witchcraft is not fear, but as we have suggested a sense of something out of place. That perception undoubtedly fits into alleged witchcraft cases old and new. Certainly there was fear on the part of those who sensed something wrong about the old (or young and too enchanting) woman with the black cat and odd look who lived down the street. Or, if not fear, at least apprehension, may accompany leaving one's children with the smiling preschool teacher who now have them in her care almost longer hours than the parent. But on another level it may have been a feeling that a world in which such persons interlope is twisted or even upside down; it violates the proper order of things that people who do strange things at night live next door, or that my children have to leave home for day-care.

We are speaking of the intrusion of something that defies classification, like weeds defined as any plant in the wrong place, or dirt as matter in the wrong place. African religion, Douglas insists, is not really based on intense dread or anxiety; the casual way rituals are performed, with much laughter and chatter, makes this clear. They are rather like a job that has to be done: to establish classifications, as when young men or women are passed into adulthood, or a purification rite is done to eradicate the 'dirt' or pollution of something spiritually in the wrong place. Witches, as marginal persons – from border areas, outcasts, in the wrong role, the mentally disturbed – are thereby suspect. But Douglas goes so far as to say that if an African felt witchcraft were being worked against him, the response would not be abject fear so much as the outrage one would feel if he found his funds were being embezzled; anger and a determination to do something about it.[26]

In *Natural Symbols*, Douglas outlines two ways of looking at social organization, which she calls grid and group. Grid refers to systems of classification which bring order to human society based on a presumed stable cosmic pattern. An example is the caste system in India, in which human society is structured as an extension of the eternal *dharma*, or cosmic pattern, and is in principle order unchanging into which an individual must fit, rather than changing the pattern to meet the individual. Group refers to social pressures and indicates how the group establishes its boundaries and constrains its members' identities: I am part of this tribe, this caste or class, this church, this nation; that's part of who I am. All societies have both grid and group, but their relative strength varies considerably, and so does their understanding of purity vs pollution, and righteousness vs sin.[27]

In societies emphasizing both strong grid and group, one finds a pronounced concern for purity, with well-defined purification rituals, since purity rules define and maintain the social structure. Sin means essentially the violation of formal rules; focus is on behaviour rather than one's internal state of being. In societies with strong group but weak grid consciousness, on the other hand, while there is concern for purity, sin is more a matter of pollution that can become lodged, like a disease, within a person or society; one's internal state is therefore important. Here, trance states may be considered dangerous since they can let in evil in the form of demonic possession, whereas in weak group societies they may be considered not dangerous, and even welcomed.[28]

While it should be emphasized again that all societies contain elements of both, by way of example it could be said that many Asian societies, such as Hindu India with its caste system or traditional Japan with its formal behaviour, as well as Catholic forms of Christianity, stress grid; the kind of African tribal society already cited, as well as evangelical or pentecostal Christianity with the importance it gives inner faith, and the characteristic desire to purify congregations and communities of deviant persons or tendencies, accentuates the maintenance of clearly-defined group boundaries.

Myth and Bonding

Here is where myth comes in. Myths are, among other roles, instruments of initiation and bonding, and thereby of assimilating persons into the grid and group mentality of a society. One way they do this is by identifying persons who are sources of evil. In formal and informal initiations into groups, telling the mythic story of the group's origin, and of significant events including the incursion of evil in its history, is a typical part of the process. Myths as the expression of a worldview and its attendant values in narrative form, can exist in many groups, and do to the present day.

Raphael Falco has written of myth as the bonding of 'charismatic groups' – groups in which the presence of other members of the group has an energizing, commitment-building power, and for which shared stories are an important facilitator of that bonding.[29] Such stories were important in the tribes of primal society, in all newly-arisen religious movements, among medieval knights who knew the tales of Roland or of King Arthur and his court, and they remain important today. Anyone who has absorbed the lore of a school, army regiment, church, street gang, of subcultures like those of gays or goths, or of a 'corporate culture', knows they have their stories, which are functionally myths in that they present certain basic values and attitudes in narrative form: this story tells how we think and how we do things in this place.

For that matter, there may well be two levels of such stories: the official ones told by the leaders, and the kinds of stories students, soldiers or workers tell when the teachers, officers or bosses aren't listening. It is fair to say that the importance of such stories in sociological understanding is increasing, as is recognition that they can profitably be analysed with the help of classic mythological studies.[30]

Not seldom these stories present intriguing echoes of how evil is perceived in classic myths: This place was good until such a person arrived on the scene, or until a certain thing happened, or the negative side of what was once a strength emerged as circumstances rearranged themselves; then it all changed. In the present study, affirming as it will the value of looking at such narratives in mythological light, contemporary subculture stories like these will have their role.

Consider the already-cited story of King Arthur. It is well known that, both in medieval sources like Mallory's *Morte d'Arthur* and the 1960 musical *Camelot*, the court of the legendary King and his knights of the Round Table enjoyed an imprecisely-dated but afterwards-remembered time when all was fair as knights went out of their often-individual quests but returned in peace – until the coming of evil with Sir Lancelot and his affair with Queen Guinevere.

As so often in myth, all was well until a certain intrusion occurred. Exactly why is not always clear; as we have seen, in myth there is always a possible backstory. In any case one salient attribute of evil is that it is non-rational, an inexplicable fracture in the smooth ordering of creation. The *Titanic* sailed peacefully and hopefully till that terrible moment. In modern myth, *The Lord of the Rings* presents the Shire as idyllic until the impingement of the Shadow from outside, and in the *Star Wars* cycle the galaxy is prosperous and peaceful until inordinate lust for power above all else leads to the rise of the Empire. Young parents of the 1980s, perhaps idealizing their own childhoods in stable families with stay-at-home moms in the 1950s, were sometimes quick to see evil lurking in their new world of absentee parents and day-care centres.

People Out of Place

One mythic source of evil, then, is persons who tear the fabric of an orderly society, opening to the dark abyss beneath or beyond it, and what that man or woman of sin represents. So it is that the pollution of evil can be attributed to witches, vampires, sorcerers, the evil eye, or similar totally malevolent but human sources, even as the defilement of Carbonek was due to the violence of Garlon and then of Balin.

What was the offence of those knights? Not that they were violent as such, for they were warriors, but that they were violent in the wrong place, and against the wrong person: Garlon had violated the standards of knighthood, which said one should be violent only to uphold honour, or in defence of the helpless, or against enemies of the lord to whom he had sworn fealty; Balin had violated hospitality, and a highly sacred place filled with deep peace.

People of the wrong kind, in the wrong place, like witches and sorcerers in the traditional sense of the word who work magic for harm, can be sources of evil. In many cultures, such as some South American,

Australian, African and Slavic societies, a great amount of everyday havoc is ascribed to such sinister individuals. Countless myths are told illustrating witchcraft and its antidotes. Indeed, in common story death is never truly natural, but always due to one of two sources: witchcraft or foolishness.

The ultimate inspiration of such evil may be beyond the circles of this world. That will be our next consideration.

Chapter 3

Space Invaders

The Other in the Führer

A great deal of sensationalistic nonsense has been written about the alleged role of occultism and demonic forces in the evil that was Nazism. But one observer whom it might not be amiss to cite is Denis de Rougemont, a French Swiss writer well regarded around the 1940s, who proposed in such elegant essays as *Le Part du Diable* (1944: 'The Devil's Share') that sceptical moderns were too quick to reject the reality of Satan, especially in light of the horrific events of that decade. De Rougemont heard Adolf Hitler speak on several occasions, and was struck by the way in which this man, who outside oratorical performance seemed so mediocre, even somewhat ridiculous, on taking the platform suddenly became something else:

> He does not belong to himself, has no specific qualities, vices or status. He is the channel through which the forces of History pass ... Hitler is sufficiently demonic to have been able to awaken our demons, through a kind of contagion, or rather of spiritual induction. His task as a *tempter* consists in depriving individuals of the sense of their moral responsibility, hence of the sense of their guilt. In fusing them into a passionate mass he exalts in the souls of the most disinherited a feeling of invincible power. He repeats to them the Devil's old slogans: 'You will not die! You will become like gods!'[31]

Here we see an oratorical channel who, despite appearances, when connected with a crowd became possessed with the force and fury of Satan, as it were giving the prince of darkness a human face. De

Rougemont wisely does not try to put the Nazi leader inside a box of words, defining him as possessed or pathological. This author recognizes that the mystery of iniquity past and present is never wholly contained within any one theory of theology or psychology. But he leaves us with an unforgettable image of irrational power breaking into twentieth-century space and time, presenting mythic allures almost as old as time.

'You Will Be like God, Knowing Good and Evil'

The original example of an outside power of evil coming into our world, or at least into a paradise within our world, is the story of the Garden of Eden in the biblical book of Genesis. We told in Chapter 2 that God made the idyllic Garden of Eden, then placed therein Adam the first man, and next shaped for him as 'helpmeet' the woman Eve from his rib. The Lord gave the man and woman the garden and all its goodly fruit to eat, but with a warning: 'You may freely eat of every tree of the garden, but of the tree of the knowledge of good and evil you shall not eat, for in the day that you eat of it you shall die.' (Gen. 2: 16–17) However an intruder into the garden had another idea:

> Now the serpent was more subtle than any other wild creature that the Lord God had made. He said to the woman, 'Did God say, "You shall not eat of any tree of the garden?" ' And the woman said to the serpent, 'We may eat of the fruit of the trees of the garden; but God said, "You shall not eat of the fruit of the tree which is in the midst of the garden, neither shall you touch it, lest you die." ' But the serpent said to the woman, 'You will not die. For God knows that when you eat of it your eyes will be opened, and you will be like God, knowing good and evil.' (Gen. 3: 1–5)

So, Eve was persuaded to eat of the fruit, and next convinced her spouse Adam to do so. Their eyes were opened. The first product of the new knowledge of good and evil was awareness that they were naked; immediately the abashed couple made themselves garments of fig leaves. The next consequence came as they concealed themselves when God came to walk in the garden in the cool of the day. Hiding was a sure sign of guilt, and before long the story came out. The serpent was cursed to crawl on his belly. Adam and Eve were expelled from the garden; he was condemned to till the ground and gain food only by the sweat of his face, and she to bring forth children in great pain.

Although this myth is known to all three Abrahamic faiths: Judaism, Christianity and Islam, Christian theology in particular has made much of it. Adam's 'fall' is said to be the source of 'original sin', that propensity for evil which has cursed humankind ever since, requiring their redemption by Christ. Moreover, the faith of Christ identified the serpent with Satan, or the Devil, the great adversary of God. The Dark Lord only began his work of leading astray human beings in the primal garden. It continues on yesterday, today and tomorrow in the Evil One's obsessive desire to ruin God's creation through human sin. The demonic labour commenced in the first book of the Bible does not end until the Beast is cast forever into the bottomless pit at the end of the last book in the (Christian) Bible, Revelation.

The traditional Satan is a great diabolical figure put together from scattered references throughout scripture, bits of Jewish and other folklore, extra-canonical apocalyptic, and the Zoroastrian model of the eternal adversary of God, Ahriman, lord of the lie, over against Ahura Mazda, Lord of Light. Theological work made it all consistent. In the end the Christian devil presents a powerful picture, above all as painted by John Milton in his great epic poem, *Paradise Lost* (1667). (It has been said that the average Englishman believes everything in *Paradise Lost* is to be found somewhere in the Bible.) Here, even before Genesis, Satan fought against heaven and was there from cast out, reaching a place of 'No light, but rather darkness visible', 'regions of sorrow, doleful shades, where peace and rest shall never dwell, hope never comes that comes to all'.

Nevertheless Satan, the great rebel against the omnipotent God, in words which some readers have found perversely appealing, declares his consciousness to be 'A mind not to be changed by place or time. The mind is its own place, and in itself can make a heav'n of hell, a hell of heav'n.' For 'To reign is worth ambition though in hell: better to reign in hell than serve in heav'n.' Thus the Enemy of Good can declare, with a touch of regret but no turning back, 'Farewell, happy fields,' and again, 'Farewell remorse: all good to me is lost; Evil, be thou my good.'

None other than this defiant and cunning rebel took form in Eden as the lowly serpent with a view to spoiling hated heaven by marring God's greatest creation. Yet even the spoiler could not but pause for a moment before Eve, his eyes almost bedazzled by her blessed beauty: 'Abashed the Devil stood, and felt how awful goodness is, and saw

Virtue in her shape how lovely.' But he continued with what he had set out to do.

The biblical and Miltonic Satan reminds us that the author of evil, though based outside the world as we ordinarily know it, is nonetheless also a part of our planet, full of feelings and even gestures not entirely inhuman, even as Hitler, though strange, was also familiar, and we do well to recognize that what was in him is also to some degree in us, though perhaps as yet not fully awakened. It is as though the alien is like a magnifying glass, enlarging and separating out for our inspection what is already here at hand though mixed in with everything else, even as alien evil can also be the lens of a burning glass, destroying what it particularly focuses on.

Iblis: He Who Would Not Worship Adam

In Islam, Shaytan (Satan; the Adversary) or Iblis (the Slanderer) is likewise a rebel against God. In the Qur'an, we are told that when God made Adam, he commanded the angels to bow down to Adam as his viceroy on earth. All complied save Iblis: 'He refused, and waxed proud, and so he became one of the unbelievers.' (Sura 2, l. 33) The Muslim scripture then proceeds to relate, more briefly than Genesis, the tale of the forbidden tree, Satan's tempting of the primal parents, and their exclusion from the garden; we noted in a previous chapter how Eden was later memorialized in Mecca.

Islamic folklore has embellished the spare Qur'anic account. Storytellers related that when Iblis first saw Allah's new creation made of nothing better than clay, and knowing that the Creator intended to make this unassuming two-legged creature higher than any other of his servants, the proud adversary kicked it with his foot till it echoed. But when Satan then puffed himself up with vainglory and declared he would never give honour to this contemptible new lord of earth and air, God in wrathful response wanted to cast the renegade angel out of heaven. But Iblis cried out, 'Give me time. Do not banish me yet. Let me tempt Adam and his sons. Then we will see if they have faith!'

Perhaps recognizing the value of testing human faith, God said he would give his challenger till the Day of Judgement to see what he could do. But Allah made it plain that after that Day of Days, Iblis would pay for his evil deeds. As in the Book of Revelation, he would be cast into a deep pit and its entry sealed over so he could do no more harm. In our middle time, though, Iblis continuously and contemptuously still entices the sons and daughters of Adam and Eve to sin against God.[32]

But in Islam the 'fall' did not result in a burden of original sin laid upon all subsequent humans. Iblis alone bears the guilt of the forbidden tree. Others carry the stain only of their own offences, though we all suffer the consequences of our race being ejected from paradise to live in a wearisome world, as we saw in Chapter 2.

The story is told of the great Sufi mystic al-Junayd, that he once met Iblis as the latter was wearing the guise of an ill-featured old man at the gateway of a mosque. Knowing him to be the Evil One, the saint asked the tempter why he would not bow down to Adam. Cleverly, the other responded, 'Junayd, how could you imagine that I should bow down to any except God?' Junayd was at first taken aback, but then a voice within told him to reply, 'You're lying – if you had been an obedient servant you would not have disobeyed His Command.' The accursed elder cried out, 'O God! You've burnt me!', and vanished.[33]

Indeed, there were Sufis who defended Iblis, regarding one who refused to worship man to be a true monotheist. Though some such misbelievers were executed as heretics, they are revered as martyrs even today by those who consider Sufi, not orthodox, Islam to be the true form of the faith.[34]

The Meaning of the Outsider Myth

Sceptical critics dismiss any explanation of evil in terms of an outside Satan as simply evading human responsibility, especially one's own. 'The devil made me do it', they say, is too easy an excuse. However, a deeper look at Satan may reveal that the devil does deal with important issues mythically. First, of course, is the 'backstory' – how is it that this is the kind of world in which we can make evil choices, and all too often do so?

Second, how do we explain natural as well as human evil? The fact is that the world itself often seems accursed – animals suffer as well as humans, and not always from human agency; disasters such as earthquake, flood and drought occur, apparently because of the kind of world, and universe, it is.

Third, and perhaps most interesting of all, the figure of Satan offers a greatly enlarged image of those human traits that lead to catastrophic consequences: the pride of Iblis and Milton's Satan, the indifference to pain in others that beliefs all too firmly fastened can cause, so that children and 'enemies' suffer for them; the inability to gaze long at that which is truly good, particularly in others, as Milton's Satan was held only for a moment by the beauty and goodness of Eve.

Yet, as we have noted, in these myths the Evil One is within as well as without the world. He comes from a higher sphere, originally angelic, but abjuring that status as his rebellion seeks revenge on God by causing as much trouble as he can here in God's creation. Other myths there are even more radical, making the creator of our particular planet himself a fallen deity.

Prisonhouse of Souls

That was the view of the ancient Gnostic forms of the Christian faith, which typically presented elaborate mythological scenarios in which earth was made by a lower 'demiurge', a divine pretender whose ambition exceeded his ability. A mere emanation from God, he nonetheless tried his hand at world-creating and bungled the job, which explains the many imperfections of his craftsmanship. We humans, or some of us, are nonetheless sparks of the divine light entrapped in shells of matter in a deeply flawed world, a dark land whose jailers are *archons*, baleful rulers of the planets visible in the night sky, who want no escapees from this prisonhouse.

No wonder we often seem lonely and lost, crying in the words of the old spiritual, 'Sometimes I feel like a motherless child.' We are exiles caught in a cruel world we never made. Only by acquiring *gnosis* or wisdom, in Christian gnosticism inner light brought by Christ as envoy from the Halls of Light far above the realm of the imperfect god, can we learn our true nature and the way out of bondage.[35]

This Gnostic myth has never really died. It was kept alive by various medieval 'heresies' such as that of the Albigensians, sorely persecuted in France. Nineteenth-century writers like the poet William Blake and the novelist Herman Melville, author of *Moby Dick*, openly espoused the Gnostic view that this world, with all its evil, must be out of the shop of an inferior maker whose hand often trembled, or who did not mean us well. For Melville, the white whale was clearly a symbol of humankind's countless quests doomed to futility in such a fallen place.

In the twentieth century something like the Gnostic myth was revived by the horror writer H. P. Lovecraft (1890–1937), whose 'Cthulhu mythos' told of powerful evil beings predating humanity on earth, who appear on the edge of our worst nightmares and terrors, and who are biding their time in hidden lairs till their hour comes round again. Lovecraft further wrote of 'the blind idiot god Azathoth, Lord of All Things, encircled by his flopping horde of mindless and amorphous dancers, and lulled by the thin monotonous piping of a demoniac flute held in nameless paws.'[36]

A few devotees of Lovecraftiana have believed, or wanted to believe, that the author was on to some strange source of knowledge, and concealed shuddery but crucial truth in his arcane tales. Of more interest to us, though, is the way contemporary young people of the 'goth' set have taken to the Cthulhu and Azathoth mythoi as, whether literally true or not, important to their worldview, expressing it as it were in narrative form. These youths, with their black garb, tormented hair, and eldritch jewellery, their fascination with blood and death, their black metal music, their vampire-like or sado-masochistic 'sacraments', are clearly aliens from the sunny world of optimists.

No doubt many or most of them have experienced life as lonely outsiders, the sort of children teased and excluded by the others, and perhaps by their families as well, able to find fellowship only with others of a like aloneness in a harsh world of little light. For them, reality shades from red to black, its tangled roots dark beyond what most can imagine, the only redemption rites of blood and near death. It is nothing strange, then, that stories of nameless terrors beneath the skin of the world, and of a blind idiot god ruling from the realm of chaos at the heart of the universe, would express what they feel.[37] The ancient myth of the Gnostic demiurge lives on, and will probably take new forms in the future.

The Gnostic myth proposed a dark world, indeed a dungeon-world within which one must find the one narrow shaft of light opening to escape. The goth Cthulhu mythos, even darker, inculcates romantic, defiant despair, or learning to enjoy the strange horrors of a perverted planet. As we will soon see, myths of the trickster, or of animals like the African toad who botched the job of bringing immortality to humankind, suggest a response perhaps wistful but overall amused at the folly that seems to be built into this particular planet. But one can also know cosmic horror and despair.

Myths Do Not Die But Change

Gnosticism, and its way back out of an evil world, offers an interesting example through which to make an important point about myth:

myths do not die so much as change. The anthropologist Claude Lévi-Strauss, in a book called *The Raw and the Cooked*, declared that a myth is composed of all its variants, across both space and time.[38] Thus presumably the modern interpretation of a myth, or a modern story based on it, is just as much 'the' myth as its ancient precedents. This important perspective brings out what is lastingly true and significant about myths in human experience. To be sure, myths, or their prototypes, had their origins in oral culture before writing; but good myth did not stop there. Myths are told over and over, in many ways, and then without dying provide themes woven into new myths, including those of stage and screen. That is all part of the mythic process. To put it another way, myths in various times and places can have a 'family resemblance' one to another, just as members of many generations or several lineages of the same family can sometimes share the family nose, smile or distinctive gesture.

(Indeed, one could say that an unchanging myth is not alive, but already no more than a relic of the past, studied in the classroom but not told on the playground or seen on the silver screen. The real myths of a society or subculture, like those of any modern youth culture, popular culture or business culture, are probably not even recognized as myths, if that word is taken to mean something from the fossilized past, or some tale that is not true. Yet such they are, insofar as they present something people need to know in narrative form.)

We have then indicated that outsider myths of evil, like all myths, function as words, ideas, images, feelings that bond within committed, charismatic groups; that they change as these groups, and the larger social milieu, change; that they evoke responses of emotion and action which, probably shared by the group, link it together against the outside world. All this is best done by a story of how evil intruded into a world otherwise idyllic, for it is being recited to people whose lives are stories, as are all of ours. We are told evil was really there from the beginning, or can be traced to a particular person or event, or to an evil deity or force: out of all this comes the feeling and the deed. We will now examine in further detail how myth can hold that evil is built into the very nature of the universe, even as it points tentatively towards roadways away from its miasma.

Chapter 4

The Way Things Are

Wrong from the Start

In some mythical views, evil is simply built into the nature of the universe as we know it. It is due to conflict between different corners of creation as the one becomes many, or death is necessary to keep the world from getting over-populated. Mythically, a violence-prone cosmos may be dramatized in the form of conflict between gods, a war which may well start as soon as the first divine children themselves emerge from the primal oneness. Or wrongness may be rooted in humanity itself, bespoken in tales of early blundering efforts at making humans, as in the Maya myth already presented, and never entirely eradicated.

In the old polytheistic religions, characteristically the problems of this world were the result of conflict between creator gods, or which emerged on the divine level within a generation or two. In ancient Egypt, although the world was generated solely by the sun-god Re, or Amon-Re, conflict broke out in the generation of his great-grandchildren Osiris, the latter's sister-wife Isis, and their disruptive elder brother Set, fomenter of chaos. Isis and Osiris had to battle long against their twisted kin, the struggle entailing the death and resuscitation of Osiris, before Set was forced out into the desert fringes of civilization, where still he wanders, seeking what he may destroy.

Recall the Maya myth telling us that the gods Hurricane and Plumed Serpent made repeated errors in creating humans. First they made them too soft, then too wooden and no more able to remember anything that a piece of furniture. Even when the human form had been more or less accomplished, people were at first unable to speak clearly, thus making them far less than human.[39] In Aztec mythology, creation was a series of five 'suns' or worlds; we are now in the fifth. Each up until that last was made by one god but destroyed by another out of jealousy; the present one endures but must be sustained by the blood of continual sacrifice.

Who Is Greatest among the Gods?

Or consider the creation myths of the Sumerians, Babylonians and Assyrians of ancient Mesopotamia. The Akkadian (Babylonian) account, according to text known as the *Enuma Elish*, goes like this. (Many scholars believe this version had some influence on the creation narrative of another Semitic people, the Hebrews, as recorded in the Book of Genesis.)

At first only infinite sea existed, no doubt signifying primordial chaos. The ocean was divided into fresh waters, embodied in the god Apsu; and salt water, the goddess Tiamat. These two deities conjoined and produced more gods in several generations. But hardly had new gods been born than the parent deities, Apsu and Tiamat, wished to destroy them, apparently fearful of their own pre-eminence in the eyes of lively younger divinities. The youthful offspring included Anu, the Heavens; Ea, an ambitious deity who aspired to replace Apsu, and did so when the latter tried to destroy the successive generations of gods; and Marduk, who was in turn superseded Ea as greatest of gods.

For her part, stormy Tiamat, dragon-goddess of the salty sea, made various monsters to devour her progeny. Understandably, the other gods of the pantheon wanted her stopped. But who was capable of that task? Ea and Anu tried, and though they were successful in displacing Apsu, even their power was not equal to containing the female fury.

Then Marduk raged against Tiamat with all the force of thunder and lightning, as well as of a magic cloak that whispered him instructions. He split her body open, thus bringing order out of chaos. One half of her he made the sky, the other half the earth. Turning to setting the world in order, he built the great city of Babylon, and made humans to be its inhabitants, and slaves of the gods.[40]

Problem Gods

The Greek creation account, according to Hesiod, also has evil, in the sense of violence, conflict and destruction, already present in its chronicle of primordial crimes before humans arrived to add their bit. Humans can and often do get caught up in jealous conflicts between gods without knowing it. (For example, the great hero Herakles or Hercules suffered from the rage of Hera because he was the child of a human mother with whom Hera's husband, Zeus, had one of his many extra-marital affairs. Though this was no fault of the boy, the anger of the incensed divine queen focused on him from infancy on up.)

As in the Valley of the Two Rivers, Hesiod's myth began with Chaos. Chaos (the word is related to our 'yawn'), a gap or empty space, was first. Into this 'yawning' appeared Gaia, the earth goddess. She was the first of the primordial gods so to emerge; others included Tartaros, the underworld, and Eros, sexual desire. Then Chaos gave birth to Night, and Gaia to Ouranos, the sky, and Pontos, the sea; from here on birth from a goddess is the normal means of creation, though as yet without male assistance.

Ouranos, however, is male, and as sky lowering over earth he mated with Gaia. They conceived twelve offspring, the Titans. But Ouranos, like Apsu and Tiamat apprehensive towards the next generation, refused to allow them to be born, but shoved them back into Gaia's womb. The earth goddess was naturally furious, and conspired with her youngest, Cronos, to defeat the father's schemes. She managed to slip him a sickle as the babe lurked within her body, and the next time Ouranos approached the goddess with sexual intent, the child castrated his father. (He threw the severed genitals into the sea, and from them emerged Aphrodite, the goddess of love and passion; Ouranos, defeated, retired to become the dome of the sky, and little more is heard of him.)

The Titans, now free to be born, emerged and themselves quickly entered upon an orgy of procreation; from their eager matings were born numerous Mediterranean islands, mountains and rivers. Cronos, marrying his sister Rhea, fathered six of the major Olympian deities, the gods Hades, Poseidon and Zeus; the goddesses Hestia, Demeter and Hera.

They did not live free, however, because Cronos – apparently learning nothing from his father's folly – tried to keep this generation of children under control by swallowing them. But mother Rhea worked out a ruse with her youngest, Zeus, to give the father a stone instead of her son to swallow, and the future king of the gods was spirited away to Crete to be raised secretly; when he was mature, he returned and induced Cronos to release his other siblings. They, together with several of Zeus' own children, became the gods of Mt Olympus.[41]

This often unpleasant narrative has been subjected to numerous interpretations ancient and modern, from seeing it as an allegory of natural processes to Freudian psychoanalytic perspectives which emphasize the obvious suggestion of Oedipus complex motifs in such scenes as a son hidden in the mother castrating his father. For now, our main stress is on what, from any human point of view, is evil, and how it occurs between gods before humans appear.

In these narratives conflict, and the evils stemming from it, are part of the very nature of the universe, existing before humans and independent of them, but inevitably ensnaring humans – and indeed the whole universe, including animals – in the strife of gods more powerful than perfect. Evils are not even the result of the insurrection of a Satan-like rebel against a perfect heaven under divine rule, even if that war in heaven took place before humans became pawns in the struggle. In the Greek heaven peace there never was, so long as gods were gods rubbing fractiously against each other in lust or anger. But other ways may be spotted in which evil was really there from the outset, perhaps involving not too many gods but one god too much alone.

The Child in the Egg

A myth from Tahiti, reflected in other 'cosmic egg' myths around the world from Greece to China, relates that at first the great god, Ta'aroa, dwelt within a round shell revolving in space. He was in deep darkness and knew nothing else, cramped and confined, perhaps for endless time. But finally, as he twisted within his shell, the encasement cracked open. He stepped out, and called above and below for anyone else, but no answer came save the echo of his own voice. As he finally broke out of darkness and confinement into sun and sea, he acted as one would expect a child to act who thought he was the only being extant, and was all-powerful: he made everything, other people included, for himself, but some were imperfect and caused disharmony.

First, he made the egg-shell into the sky. Then, working feverishly out of his anger at being so long imprisoned, he moulded mountains and clouds, earth and living beings from his own body as he tore himself apart in the rage he could now finally express. Now, alone in his own world, the all-powerful child felt himself master of everything. Then Ta'aroa wanted others, like him but subservient to him.

He made gods, first of all Tu, to be his companion in creation, then the first man and woman, Ti'i and Hina. For a while all were at peace, but conflict broke out soon enough among these spiteful gods and humans. Angered by anger on the part of those they had made in anger, Ta'aroa and Tu, abetted by Ti'i, cursed their creation. But Hina preserved as much of it as she could, for she was life-giving maiden-mother. Ti'i himself said that Ta'aroa loves to slay, but Hina loves to bring back to life, as the flowers return in the spring. So it is that though evil weighs down the world, it is kept in balance.[42]

No great psychological intuition would be required to deduce that the anger Ta'aroa expressed against himself and then against the creation, had its genesis in the long eternities he had spent enclosed in his small dark shell. No one had put him there, so far as he was aware, so there was no external object against which to vent his rage. He struck out against whatever was at hand, beginning with himself. In this sense evil tormented the god even before he undertook human creation, and much of his rage was then emptied into that creation. But he could not twist all, for the nature of life itself (Hina) set limits to divine wrath.

Full Basket of Life and Pale Fox

Another cosmic egg, also mythic, involves the divine twin theme. According to the Dogon people of Mali, in the beginning Amma, the supreme God, placed the seeds of two sets of twins, each set male and female, inside an egg.

But one of the males, Ogo, became disturbed, fearing that Amma would not give him his female counterpart after the anticipated long gestation of sixty years. The impatient prince broke violently out of the shell, trying to take his consort with him. But Amma, foreseeing the rebellion, had already removed her. Now Ogo, in complete rage, broke all the rules. He tried to create his own world, stole seeds intended to fructify the earth, and tried to utter sacred words. He even tried to mate with the earth, making her his spouse. But in all this he failed, not truly knowing divine secrets, and his efforts only made the planet dry and barren.

Finally Amma determined to counter Ogo's disastrous regimen. The only way he could do so was to sacrifice Ogo's innocent brother, Nommo. He strangled him, then scattered the pieces of his body through the cosmos, and after five days gathered them back, and restored Nommo to life. He made this righteous brother ruler of the universe; from his parts were also made the ancestors of humanity. Amma then dispatched Nommo and the ancestors down to earth in a great basket, laden with all that would be needed to sustain humanity; all plants and animals, together with the essentials of society and culture.

Amma at the same time transformed Ogo into an animal called Pale Fox. This mysterious beast, always in revolt, wanders the earth in hopeless search of his female soul, but remains always incomplete. Yet his tracks, left as he wanders, bespeak certain mysteries of life perhaps best known by souls incomplete and unfulfilled, and can be read by Dogon diviners.[43]

Here conflict began in the beginning, before humankind fully appeared; yet in this fairly optimistic story, is basically resolved by the time human society takes full form. But a remembrance of primal conflict still lingers in the form of a pale creature ever wandering the fringes of society, forever searching yet also possessed of his own kind of dark wisdom.

Repetition Universe

Here is a creation myth from India. The god Vishnu is sleeping on the coils of the thousand-headed serpent Sesha ('remainder') or Ananta ('unending') as the giant reptile floats on the infinite cosmic ocean. Then, when it is time to make the universe again, Vishnu awakes, and a lotus grows out of his navel. Brahma, the creator god, emerging from the spreading flower, proceeds actually to construct the world. When he has finished that mighty work he, together with his consort Sarasvati, and Vishnu's wives Lakshmi and Bhudevi, ascend to the highest heaven overlooking the earth, there to reign over all. Only when evil multiplies here below does the sovereign god descend, to appear in earth as an avatar, such as Rama or Krishna, to correct wrong and put the planet back in the way of Dharma or righteousness.[44]

Evils do multiply, for Vishnu's creation goes through a series of four stages, from a golden age to the last and worst state, the Kaliyuga. Then people are short-lived and out for only gain. At its end comes the last avatar of Vishnu, Kalki, a giant warrior with a flaming sword astride a white horse, who will save those who can still be saved. After his day the world will dissolve of the corrosive power of its own evil, its constituent parts becoming the Sesha, the serpentine couch of the sleeping god. This process of creation and destruction has happened over and over, an infinite number of times in the past and will presumably recur infinitely in the future. Though details may vary, and the scenario may be put in the context of larger and larger cycles, the general pattern of an endless pattern of creation and destruction can be found throughout Hinduism, Buddhism and Jainism.

Clearly, the upshot is that evil is a built-in part of the universe from non-beginning to non-end, since it appears mandatory that each cycle go through its ages of evil as well as of good, even though the mess is always cleaned up and the universe starts fresh once more. One can compare this tremendous vision with that of the philosopher Friedrich Nietzsche's idea of eternal recurrence: if time is truly infinite, he said, then everything that ever happened must be eventually repeated, not once but an infinite number of times. He or she who can affirm all those numberless returns of one's life with joy is truly brave and wise. Donald S. Fryer, a poet perhaps inspired by this awesome notion, wrote of Mycenae, city of King Agamemnon, leader of the Greeks in the Trojan War:

> It may be that no splendor passes evermore from Earth,
> But that, through endless incantations – subtle, strange, divine –
> It knows in far-off time and space a new resplendent birth:
> In what age, in what world, shall this proud lion find again –
> Deep in the sea of stars – his race of gods and godlike men?[45]

Let it be recalled that the Trojan War was not only heroic, but also that Homer did not shrink from describing its many ghastly atrocities on both sides, and that Agamemnon was of the terrible house of Atreus. The many appalling deeds of this dysfunctional family, including the murder of Agamemnon by his wife Clytemnestra upon his return from battle, were the frequent subject-matter of the great Athenian tragedians. We see then that in affirming eternal recurrence or repetition we are not only celebrating the joy of unending life, but also the bloodshed that stains it, and the acts of heroism and villainy that make it a drama greater than the life or death of any of the players.

The Twin Sons of Endless Time

Still another possibility is a dualism of good and evil principles, like God and Satan, but which has existed virtually forever and will exist so long as endless time lasts. The closest one comes to this idea in a historical religion is perhaps Zurvanism, which may have occurred in Iran prior to Zoroastrianism, and which was incorporated into some philosophical expressions of the latter faith, though in its orthodox form the cosmic conflict was limited to 9,000 years.

Mythically, Zurvan, whose name means 'endless time', save for his wife was a solitary deity in the beginning, before the creation of heaven and earth. He desired a son, and to this purpose offered sacrifices for a millennium, though he doubted whether they would be honoured. But in fact his wife gave birth to twins, Ahura Mazda and Ahriman, the first representing his faith, the second his doubt. Zurvan had reportedly decreed that the firstborn would rule the universe; hearing this, the second ripped his way out of the womb and demanded his birthright as well. Ahura Mazda, the Lord of Light, became the good God, and Ahriman his equal opponent, until the end of the age when the better twin would triumph.[46]

Despite the conditioning of Zurvanism by the need in a monotheistic religion for righteousness to prevail, the idea of an eternal dualism built into the universe and its spiritual nature remains intriguing. It was developed to a more absolute point in Manichaeism, a religion strongly influenced by Zoroastrianism, which spread from Europe to China in the early centuries CE. According to mythical doctrine preached by the prophet Mani (216–277 CE), in beginningless time two roots or principles have always coexisted, light or good, and darkness or ignorance. Darkness is always divided against itself, and so continually strife-ridden and chaotic. The two realms were long separated, but in the present age have become commingled, so that light and darkness must struggle for ultimate control of the universe. In the end of our age, they will be separated again, but will forever continue to coexist, each in its own place.[47]

Mircea Eliade tells a folktale involving God and Satan from his native Romania. This story is found in variants throughout southeast Europe, and seems to be ultimately of Manichean and Zoroastrian derivation, through the former's medieval Bogomile descendant. It seems that before the creation of the world nothing there was but infinite sea, above which God and Satan dwelt together. Both appear to have existed since beginningless time, but God in some manner was superior to Satan; only he could create. When God then decided to create the world, he sent Satan to dive into the depths of the sea and bring up the 'seed' of land. He was told to do so in the name of God, but the lesser immortal invoked instead his own name, and the mud slipped through his fingers when he brought it to the surface. Finally, the third time he took up soil in both his own name and God's; this time enough remained under his fingernails for God to use. The Deity made himself a mound of earth, and there he lay down to rest. Satan, thinking his companion was asleep, had the idea of pushing him into the water to drown, and so that he alone would then be master of earth. But the more the devil rolled God towards the water's edge, the more land appeared under him, on and on until vast expanses of earth had replaced the primordial sea, and the evil one had to recognize the futility of his project.[48]

In this intriguing story both God and Satan are 'twins', equal and of unknown origin. Both have the 'trickster' quality of wanting to fool the other. Yet God had the edge; his stratagems work and the other's do not. But one senses this battle of wits will go on for a long time.

Moving up to the present, popular entertainment recalls to the classic 'evil twin' myth over and over. A *Star Trek* episode, 'The Alternative Factor', shows a pathetic/heroic figure forever wrestling in space with his anti-matter brother, each knowing that if either one got final supremacy over the other, all would be destroyed. In the TV series *Bewitched* Samantha Stevens had an evil twin sister, Serena. In *I Dream of Jeannie*, another glamorous modern witch narrative, Jeannie likewise had an unnamed evil twin sister. The evil twin to *Sabrina the Teenage Witch* was Katrina, and in the episode 'The Wish' of *Buffy the Vampire Slayer* we see a parallel universe in which Buffy Summers never came to Sunnydale. In the subsequent episode 'Doppelgangland', a vampire is transported to the 'real' Sunnydale for a classic evil twin plotline. The idea of parallel universes, suggested as possible realities by some of the more cutting-edge ideas of cosmology and physics, is becoming a staple of speculative fiction, and an ideal medium for exploring dualistic, yet built-into-the-universe interpretations of good and evil.

These are mythic narratives that make both good and evil, as humans understand them, factored into the fabric of the universe as it is. It may be, however, that in such a universe man is not the measure of all things, and that from a different perspective, those energies that seem to us evil would have another meaning, or perhaps no meaning at all.

Chapter 5

Couldn't It Have Happened Differently?

The Cosmic Joker

Something unexpectedly goes wrong, perhaps something seemingly trivial, but with big consequences. A common occurrence in myth. Quite often, myths of this type have a darkly humorous tone, as though evil were the work of what Charles Fort, a collector of bizarre phenomena, called the 'Cosmic Joker'. Often they involve the origin of death, closely related to evil in human experience.

Here are a few examples. Sir James Frazer tells us that in a myth from Sulawesi (Celebes), Indonesia, the Creator lowered from heaven to the first humans two gifts on ropes, a stone and a banana. Understandably, they rejected the stone as useless and took the fruit. Then a voice from heaven said, 'Because you have chosen the banana, your life shall be like its life. Had you taken the stone, you would have been like it, changeless and immortal.'[49]

An African creation story offers another wryly amusing tale about the origin of evil and death. Time and again on that often-troubled yet as often resilient continent, one encounters a spirit that seems to say, if we can't do anything about the human situation and its tragedies, why not just laugh instead of weep? Perhaps it is all a big joke, or a big comic mistake of some ridiculous kind. Take for example the common myth of the failed messenger to explain human death.

Here is a version from Sierra Leone. It was noted by the Limba people that the snake could avoid death just by changing his skin. Afterwards, he looked bright and fresh as new. So, people said that originally humans were supposed to have been able to rejuvenate themselves the same way. But something went wrong.

What happened? First we have to meet Kanu, the Limba creator and High God. At the beginning, this all-competent and kindly deity had lived on earth among people and animals, but withdrew to heaven because the animals refused to stop quarrelling when he asked them to make peace. While still on earth, Kanu had intended for both humans and animals not to die. He made a medicine that would prevent death. The deity gave part of it to the snake, and it worked for him. Kanu then handed a bowl containing the rest of the elixir to the snake, telling him to take it to the Limba.

But the toad objected, saying the snake moved so fast he would spill it. Toad insisted on taking it himself, even though Kanu asked him not to. Nonetheless the amphibian put the vessel on his head, apparently in no great awe of this god who seems more like part of the world than above it. Toad then started hopping, and when he hopped the second time the fluid of life all spilled. Kanu refused to make more owing to the disobedience of the toad, and for that reason all people and animals die, except the snake, who dies only if someone kills him.[50]

One can imagine a story like this being told to great comic effect by a skilful narrator. It would probably be a mistake to think that the Limba people believed this tale in quite the same way certain modern fundamentalists believe their doctrines. Rather, what it does is set a certain feeling-tone towards death and its beginning: at once wistful over what might have been, yet also humorous, as though saying, in any case let's just go ahead through life with a good sense of humour.

Other common versions of the 'failed messenger' myth in Africa involve the chameleon, thought to be very slow and dilatory compared to other animals. He is entrusted with the message of life, while another speedier envoy, such as the lizard, bears a message of mortality. Naturally the latter arrives first, and human beings have to die. Or, as among the Igbo, the animal messengers, both dog and sheep, not only are delayed by a desire to eat, but get the message garbled so that, though it was meant to convey immortality, it came out to mean death.[51] The theme is persistent: some little mistake, or some small and not-too-bright creature who, doing what his kind usually does, fell down on the job, made the difference between eternal life and death for humanity.

Fatal Mistakes

Sometimes death and its attendant evil is the fault of a single person, often a woman, whose inordinate greed or curiosity brings it about.

We have already considered the story of Eve, persuaded to taste a forbidden but irresistible fruit, then taking it to her husband. In Greek mythology Pandora was the first woman, according to Hesiod's *Works and Days*; her name means 'Many Gifts'. But though her charms made her wholly captivating to men, she was sent not as a benign gift to those of male gender but to harass them, some say as punishment from Zeus for man's impiety.

That view undeniably reflects the low view of women characteristic of Greek civilization. That ancient culture, for all its glories, was very much a man's world in which women were expected only to keep house and produce children, it was hoped male. (Yet on the other hand in Greek mythology goddesses like Hera, Aphrodite and Athena were powerful, often the protectors of mighty warriors. For that matter some classicists have recently pointed out that in many of the great comedies and tragedies, perhaps reflecting real life, women find ways to exercise more independence and power than one might have expected. Yet the paradox of low status for women on earth and powerful goddesses in heaven is widespread; compare also India and Japan.)

Pandora was indeed endowed with many gifts: beauty by Aphrodite, a thievish nature by Hermes, and a jar which contained innumerable evils that she was supposed to keep sealed, but which she could not resist opening. As she peeked in, out of it flew the plagues of war, famine and disease which have afflicted humankind ever since; only Hope remained in the jar as our sole comfort.[52]

An Australian Aboriginal myth, like those of Eve and Pandora of beginning times, and indeed with resonances of the Garden of Eden, tells us that the first people were forbidden to approach a certain hollow tree in which bees were hiving. The men observed this prohibition, but one woman was so eager to get at the honey that she chopped at the tree with an axe. Those blows released a great black bat, and that flying beast was none other than Death himself. From then on humankind has had to live under the shadow of his wings.

An African myth bespeaks the first Bugandan queen and her forgetfulness. When Nambi, consort of the great founder of the Bugandan royal line, and her husband were being lowered down from heaven to establish their kingdom on earth, the gods told them expressly not to delay. But halfway down, Nambi realized she had forgotten grain to feed her chickens, and insisted on going back to get it. In that lost moment of time Death was able to catch up with her and her companions. He has dwelt with humanity ever since.[53]

The basic point of myths like these, apart from the unfortunate tendency to blame the woman, is that the line between a perfect and an imperfect world is very fine. Some little thing could push it one way or the other. In fact, it was always seemingly small accidents or slips of mind that tilted human life in the direction of evil and death.

No doubt these stories imply a reproach to whatever powers there be that to make so much ill, even death itself, stem from such small indiscretions is unfairness on a cosmic level: people chose the banana over the stone without full disclosure of consequences, or fairly innocent curiosity or eagerness to eat led to results far beyond what anyone could have imagined at the time. But then these were the mythic times of the beginning, when everything was bound to have vast implications. After all, the whole pattern of cosmic and human life was being set up.

Turtle Island

Here is a Huron myth (similar to an Iroquois version), which indicates the vast consequences of a single accident, and includes the good and evil twin motif presented in the last chapter. In the beginning what was to become our world was, as in so many other myths, nothing but endless ocean, though populated by innumerable animals and birds of the kind that frequent the sea. Over it, above the sky, was an upper world more like ours. One day a woman of that world fell, or was pushed (some say by her husband, angry at her pregnancy) through a hole in the sky, and tumbled down to the watery realm below. Luckily, she was seen and caught by two loons; their loud haunting cry attracted other creatures, including a huge turtle who agreed to take the woman on his back.

Realizing she would need earth to make a world on the tortoise's shell, other animals dove deep into the sea to try to bring up mud – the 'earth diver' theme found in many myths. All were unsuccessful, some even staying under so long they died, until the toad managed to retrieve a bit of mud. So she made herself finally a vast country, the 'Turtle Island' of Native American lore.

In the meantime, it turned out the woman who fell from the sky was pregnant with twins. They quarrelled and fought with each other in the womb. Eventually one was born in the usual manner, but the other, the evil twin, refused normal birth, and ripping his mother's side open came out that way, killing her in the process. (From the Great

Mother's remains came all sorts of vegetables, from maize and beans to pumpkins.)

Those primal twin boys were not ordinary people, but supernatural beings whose task was to prepare the earth for human habitation. But, one being good and the other evil (why is not explained), their labours were two-sided. The first job was to make animals. The good brother made the innocent and useful beasts, while the bad one made the likes of gigantic serpents, wolves, bears and mosquitoes as big a turkeys. The good brother, going to the other's domain in search of water, could not destroy these monstrosities, but reduced them in size. The two brothers finally quarrelled to the death. The good son killed his brother, who went to the far west, where he would thereafter receive the dead into his kingdom.[54]

In the Iroquois version, the good twin made everything that is beautiful: rolling hills, lakes, flowers, gentle animals. His opposite made everything otherwise: jagged cliffs, thorns, rampaging rivers, predator animals. Right-Hand, as the good one was called, was always truthful and good-hearted; Left-Hand full of lies, violence and crime.

Right-Hand made human beings, so their nature is ultimately good. But Left-Hand insisted on playing his part as well, and introduced humans to sorcery, cruelty and aggression. In the Iroquois version also the good brother killed his brother, tossing the other's body over the edge of the world, into the next level down, the underworld. But Sky Grandmother was angry, and threw the dead twin's head into the heavens, where it became the moon. Now Right-Hand rules the day and Left-Hand the night and the underworld. The Iroquois believed these two brothers must be kept in balance; that is expressed in ritual and dance. In festivals, day activities honour Right-Hand; night ceremonies do homage to Left-Hand.[55]

Rage against Limits

In the Hopi myth of creation, people rebelled against the harmonious limits set them by the Creator, wanting more, and so fought against each other. Originally, we are told, there was only the god Taiowa, and endless space. This deity created his 'nephew', Sotuknang, who in turn made a nine-tiered world. Then Spider Woman, their next creation, filled these ample spaces with living things, culminating in people made of earths of four colours. These human experiments have moved up through successive levels of the world as they have matured, and at the same time became infected with evil by always wanting more.

At first, despite wearing skins of various tints and speaking words of diverse tongues, they felt as one and understood one another in their silences. Likewise birds and beasts felt themselves nurselings of Mother Earth, who gave them freely the county of her grains and fruit; and all that dwelt on her bosom were as one, people and animals.

But then, it is said, they forgot the commands of the Creator about harmony, and more and more began to think only of earthly things, and to see differences. People drew away from each other, and from animals. A talking bird and then a talking snake came among them, saying things that led people to be suspicious, and to accuse one another. Before long they were warlike, and then they were fighting. By the time they had emerged to the second world, despite the fact they had enough for all real needs, they began to want more. More and more they traded for things they didn't need, and the more goods they got, the more they wanted. Nonetheless, still there were a few people in each village 'who sang the song of their creation'.[56]

Can a God Be Too Beautiful?

Orpheus, in Greek mythology, son of Apollo and the muse of poetry and music, Calliope, was a poet and musician who was not only the perfection of physical beauty himself, but could play the lyre wonderfully enough to enchant gods, people, animals and even rocks with the sound of his magical melodies. As a member of Jason's party in search of the Golden Fleece, he was of help as he played while the ship *Argo* sailed through the clashing rocks and past the Sirens.

Orpheus married the dryad or nymph Eurydice, but lost her on his wedding day in this manner. A certain beekeeper named Aristaeus had tried to rape her on that auspicious and awful occasion; as she ran trying to escape, she stepped on a snake which bit and killed her. Distraught by Eurydice's death, Orpheus went to the underworld to recover his bride. His music so charmed Hades and Persephone, king and queen of the dark realm, that they promised he could take Eurydice, provided he did not look at her until they had reached the upper world. But, besotted by her beauty, the divine lover could not resist temptation, stole a glance at his wife and lost her a second time.

In his sorrow, Orpheus wandered disconsolately around Thrace. There he encountered the Maenads, women dedicated to Dionysos (also called Bacchus), god of wine and traditionally associated with frenzy and non-rational excess. The Maenads, rampaging through the mountains and woods far from home, entranced with Dionysian frenzy, were said to play with serpents and suckle animals at their breasts, and no less to tear animals and even humans apart in their fervour, eating their flesh.

Dionysos represents far more than just potent drink. He is a divine representative of everything that is Other to an orderly, stable and well-defined sacred world. In Nietzsche's famous contrast of Dionysian and Apollonian principles, this mysterious god was the polar opposite of Orpheus' well-poised father, Apollo.[57] Dionysos is all that comes unexpected and elusive; he blurs all boundaries between real and unreal, sane and mad or fantastic, human and animal, male and female; by his unique magic, he can make reality whatever he wants it to be. In Euripides' play *The Bacchae* (another name for the Maenads) Dionysos appears – whether for real or as another of his illusions – as a new god, and mercilessly abuses those who refuse to believe in such a divine novelty. For indeed Dionysos is in no particular set place, but is here, there, everywhere and nowhere, present yet just out of sight. His kind of world can be concocted by drink, drugs or ecstasy; he may be a joke, or he may be the tip of a very profound truth, welcome or not, about our universe of appearances. He could mean a golden age of spontaneity and freedom, without rules, or he could mean the free expression of the basest and cruelest impulses, without rule or restraint.[58]

Walter Otto reminds us that 'We should never forget that the Dionysiac world is, above all, a world of women. Women awaken Dionysus and bring him up. Women accompany him wherever he is. Women await him and are the first ones to be overcome by his madness.'[59] The Maenads were enthusiasts of this deity. (The word 'enthusiasm' literally means 'possessed by a god' in Greek.) They were filled with Dionysus, indeed were none other than he in human flesh. Then they encountered Orpheus, son of Apollo (his opposite, of a transcendentally balanced, sculpted male beauty), and found the master of music and measure wandering sadly in the hills, alone. What was to stop them, in their rage against order and limits, from tearing him to pieces?

Yet it is said that the pieces of his body were gathered up by the muses, and that his head and lyre continued singing and playing after all else was gone; they floated to the island of Lesbos, where they were dedicated to Apollo.

Rage against limits, though it can be a quest for freedom, makes also for evil.

Chapter 6

Trickster's Gameplan

What Is a Trickster?

In cultures around the world, a favourite character appearing in media from folk tales to modern comic strips is the perverse yet often charming, and certainly fascinating, individual who is just out for himself. This lively fellow delights in playing tricks on others, either to advantage himself or just for the sport of it. In the Old World one thinks of figures like Till Eulenspiegel in Germany, Reynard the Fox in France, Nasr-eddin the cleric/clown in Turkey.

In the Native American cultures of the New World, and also as represented by ancient mythological personages such as the Germanic Loki or, in some roles, the Greek Hermes or Hindu Krishna, the Trickster, as these figures are commonly called, was typically a more serious personage. Usually an animal in the Americas (though capable of shape shifting) – Coyote, Raven, Rabbit, Spider-man, Blue Jay – he not only played tricks but was also a culture-hero, capable of bringing great gifts to humanity, like Prometheus in defiance of Zeus. Indeed, the mystery of the Trickster lies in the way he acts entirely out of himself, being bound by no law, neither a moral code nor the Miltonic Satan's 'Evil be thou my good', yet can bring benevolence as well as bane. He is good or bad, male or female, animal or human, material or spiritual, as he feels like it, in his mysterious heart a union of opposites.

The Native American Trickster is virtually co-creator of the planet, a companion of the original Creator, but one who always wants to modify the world or human society to make it more interesting. Chancy and treacherous, yet also amusing, he manages to fabricate a more intriguing as well as more difficult and dangerous world out of his insatiable curiosity and his half-baked schemes. Like the Satan of the Book of Job, or Eliade's Romanian folktale, he is there alongside God, eager to test divine perfection with his tricks and games.

The Trickster is thus human nature right there at the beginning, with all the grandeur and pathos, strength and weakness, virtue and sinfulness of which the species is capable. Because of him, the world is more fascinating than flat-out perfection would be, but also full of evil and suffering. Yet he lives outside human civilization, able to maintain the perspective of the amused, occasionally soft-hearted outsider.

Take for example the Zuni myth of the sun and moon in a box. Here the Trickster is Coyote; his companion, Eagle, while not the Creator, embodies the zenith in Zuni cosmology, and clearly represents the principle of stability and order which so neatly contrasts with the Trickster spirit.

It was near the beginning, when the world was still soft and new, and as yet neither sun nor moon lit the sky. Eagle and Coyote were out hunting together. They came to a Pueblo where the Kachinas, or nature spirits, were dancing, and they noticed something intriguing. The Kachinas had a square box. Within it were the sun and moon. When they wanted a great deal of light, they would open it and take out the sun; when only a little light was required, they would extract the moon from it.

The two hunters were amazed. Coyote wanted to steal the box, but Eagle said that would be wrong; they should just borrow it instead. That they did, and Eagle flew off with the box, while Coyote followed him on the ground. After a while, Coyote asked to be allowed to carry the box for a time instead. Eagle, mistrusting his companion, refused, saying that the other would not be able to resist the temptation of opening the box.

But Coyote continued to insist, saying his wife and children would no longer respect him if he were deemed unworthy to share the honour of carrying this treasure. Finally Eagle relented, making the animal swear he would neither drop nor open it. Coyote promised, but of course his curiosity got the better of him; he fell back, hid behind some bushes, and opened the box.

Quickly, the sun darted out and went to the edge of the sky; the world grew cold, leaves turned brown, icy winds raged, and when the moon sped out of the box also snow came down to cover the mountains and plains as well. Eagle sadly remarked to Coyote, 'If it had not been for you, sun and moon would be close and we would have had summer all the time'. Now winter and suffering had come to the world, not because Coyote was thoroughly evil so much as that he was impulsive, insatiably curious, and irresponsible, unable to think ahead to the consequences of his actions.

Loki

Many were the tales told about Loki in the great halls of old northern Europe. This son of giants was nimble, quick-witted, but an inveterate mischief-maker who varied his pattern of evil with just enough good to be truly crazy-making. It is said that once as an act of mischief Loki cut off the beautiful golden hair of Sif, wife of Thor. That outraged the god so much he would have killed Loki had he not found two skilled craftsmen from among the dwarfs who made her new hair of real gold, and in addition constructed a ship for the god Freyr and a spear for Odin.

But Loki couldn't stop troublemaking. Continuing his capricious activities, Loki determined to bring in two more dwarfs to compete with the first set. The idea was to see which pair could do the more beautiful work, and the Trickster-god wanted to make it more piquant by a wager. Loki bet on the first team. The projects were now a golden boar for Freyr, and the golden ring Draupnir for Odin. But then Loki had to cheat; he hindered the work of the two he had gambled against by becoming a fly, stinging those dwarfs as they laboured over their fine goldsmithery, thus leaving the products imperfect. Nonetheless, the gods declared them fine enough, and Loki lost his game.

In another of his uncertain moods, Loki had worked on behalf of the high gods at the time the Aesir retained giants to build for them their stronghold, Asgard. Odin and his companions had promised the huge workmen the goddess Freyr, plus the sun and moon, if they finished the work by winter, being quite sure that would not happen. But the giants had the aid of a marvellous horse, Svadifari, with whose help they were practically finished ahead of schedule. Loki played a trick on them by turning himself into a mare, whose charms so distracted the stallion that he forgot about work. The project missed the deadline, saving the gods their onerous payment. While still a mare Loki gave birth to the eight-legged steed Sleipnir, the finest horse ever, who became Odin's mount.

Loki worked against the gods, however, in his cruellest trick. The gentle and beautiful god Balder, lord of light and the sun, seems to have particularly aggravated Loki. Balder had been tormented by terrible dreams of death, and to calm him his mother Frigga, wife of Odin, caused all the elements of creation, from fire and metal to plants and animals, to swear they would not harm the innocent deity. Indeed, for amusement the gods threw things at Balder, knowing he could not be hurt. But Frigga overlooked the mistletoe, thinking it too small and obscure. Hearing this, Loki made a dart of that plant, and gave it to the blind god Hodur, guiding him so that he threw it in the direction of Balder. The projectile hit the mark; the lovely god fell dead.

Then the gods pleaded with Hela, goddess of death, to let Balder return to life. Ordinarily that dark mother keeps what she has, but she finally consented to release Balder if all beings, none excepted, would mourn for him. All did, save one old hag, who refused; some ancient commentators affirmed she was none other than Loki himself in disguise, the Trickster still vengeful against innocence and beauty. But the gods took their own vengeance against the erratic godling, who this time had gone too far, by binding Loki and confining him underground, where his writhing causes earthquakes.[60]

The African American Trickster

African American folklore has retained some of trickster-like concepts of deity we have noted in Africa. Here, for example, is how the eminent black author, Zora Neale Hurston, just after describing her mother's death, conjured the subject as a whole:

> The Master-Maker, in His making had made Old Death . . . Made him with a face that reflects the face of all things, but neither changes itself, nor is mirrored anywhere. Made the body of death out of infinite hunger. Made a weapon for his hands to satisfy his needs. This was the morning of the day of the beginning of things.
> But Death had no home and he knew it at once.
> 'And where shall I dwell in my dwelling?' Old Death asked, for he was already old when he was made.
> 'You shall build you a place close to the living, yet far out of the sight of eyes . . . For your hunger, I give you the first and last taste of all things.'[61]

Nonetheless tricksters here below get the better of death, or think they can. A trickster-figure common in African American folktales is simply called John, or Jack; her is a story Hurston tells about him going back to slavery time, in which he ran faster than Ole Massa, and maybe even than death. It seems that John had been praying to God to take him to heaven right away, so tired was he of his hard life. He pleaded with God to come down in his fiery chariot and carry him away. One night Ole Massa was passing by John's shack and heard him praying thus, and decided to test him. Massa put a bed sheet over his head, and knocked on John's door.

John quit prayin' and ast: 'Who dat?'
Ole Massa say: It's me, John, de Lawd, done come wid my fiery chariot to take you away from this sin-sick world.

But John changed his mind, and hid under the bed. Finally his wife Liza made him come out, and John made further excuses: he had to put on his Sunday shirt and pants, and finally begged the Lord to step further and further back, so the bright radiance of the divine countenance would not scorch him.

Ole Massa stepped back a step or two mo' and out dat door John come like a streak of lightning. All across de punkin patch, thru de cotton over de pasture – John wid Ole Massa right behind him. By de time dey hit the cornfield John was way ahead of Ole Massa.
Back in de shack one of the de children was cryin and she ast Liza: 'Mama, you reckon God's gointer ketch papa and carry him to Heben wif him?'
'Shet yo' mouf, talkin' foolishness!' Liza clashed at de chile. 'You know de Lawd can't outrun yo' pappy – specially when he's barefooted at dat.'[62]

The story stops here, but given the conditions of slavery, one wonders what the eventual effect of John's runaway would have been on his family and the plantation. The Trickster's dash in one direction can leave imprints in another; he is the original master of unintended consequences. The main point is that, literally in this case, the Trickster is found where a door opens, and one can see stars or a wide horizon; what comes in or goes out seems to depend on the wind as well as the Trickster's will, for he personifies the universe's uncertainty principle.

Queens and Jokers: The Trickster Today

Signs abound that the Trickster, both in his role as culture-creator and as disruptive source of evil, has as much a place in the modern world as ever. Mark Thompson, a historian of 'gay' culture, points out that, while homosexuals may have been held in contempt in recent Western society, in many traditional societies 'those who bridged the genders were placed in a position of honor and ritual purpose'. He cites many instances in which such ambiguous and inclusive persons were especially valued as healers, magic-workers, or shamans.[63] (It might be noted that some classic mythic tricksters have been capable of turning themselves into females on occasion, or one might even say were transgendered. We have noted that Loki made himself into a mare to distract the giants' workhorse and give birth to Odin's Sleipnir. Some stories exist, especially among the Pueblo, in which Coyote is female; she is exceptional in that she claims to want the things she covets not for herself but for her children, and will use trickery to obtain boons for that good purpose.[64])

Going on to speak of cross-dressing 'drag queens' as contemporary tricksters, Thompson comments, 'The role of the fool, the trickster, the *contrary one* capable of turning a situation inside out, is one of the most enduring of all archetypes . . . It is a role that seems particularly suited to gay men, and in San Francisco it is possible to trace a succession of such men playing the role with glee.'[65] Yet it is significant that Thompson's point is he is describing a moment in gay culture just before the fall, as it were, just before the coming of AIDS and the pall it cast over a time which, in retrospect, seemed a world of humour and delight in its very perversity.

Suddenly something like a fatal accident erupted, a door was slammed shut, and instead of light-hearted self-mockery serious rage against limits combined with inner despair. The Trickster became the mocker, and a symbol of paradise lost. Sacvan Bercovitch wrote of three levels of the Trickster: innocent, satirical and sinister.[66] The 'drag queen', strictly as a symbol, could be said to have moved through the three: innocent fun; satirizing the attitudes of society; image of a lifestyle that had become bearer of dread disease.

The same process may be seen in women in the role. Ricki Stefanie Tannen, in *The Female Trickster*, gives as positive examples women in fiction from Fanny Price in Jane Austen's *Mansfield Park* to the teenage sleuth Nancy Drew, who while quite different in many ways have in common such trickster traits as accepting as adaptive colouring the social roles expected of women, while inwardly looking at things from an independent angle, often with a sense of humour, seeing much that conformists from flatfooted policemen to self-important adults overlook, in the end making something new out of the mix. For, Tannen says, 'Tricksters preside over moments of passage, rupture, and transformation. Tricksters appear to model change and possibilities.'[67]

Take for example Martha Jane Cannery (1852–1903), the Old West legend known as 'Calamity Jane'. A nonconformist all her life, according to her own not-always-reliable account Jane came to West with her family in 1865, hunting and riding with the men along the way, and becoming an excellent shot and horsewoman. By 1870, she was a scout for the army, serving such figures as General Custer, wearing the male uniform of a soldier. She performed heroically on some occasions; one account is that she got her nickname when she saved the life of a Captain Egan in a disastrous skirmish, and this officer said afterwards, 'I name you Calamity Jane, the heroine of the plains.' Others say she won the moniker because her reputation was such that men of the frontier said to get involved with her was to 'court calamity'. By 1875 she settled in Deadwood, South Dakota, where her activities included bartending, prostitution and her famous friendship with Wild Bill Hickok. After Hickok was killed during a poker game in 1876, Jane reportedly went after his murderer, Jack McCall, with a meat cleaver. Calamity's later highly varied activities ranged from saving passengers on a stagecoach attacked by Plains Indians to appearing in Buffalo Bill's famous Wild West show.

This tale, and there is much more, speaks for itself as the saga of a trickster-like figure, playing many roles, wearing many garbs, on all sides of moral values, like Loki acting out of herself and her own moods rather than any conventional values.

The Joker and the Sociopath

A trickster-like figure familiar to many contemporaries is the Joker, a character in several DC Comics tales (first introduced as long ago as 1940), and above all in Batman adventures including the famous Batman movies; in *The Dark Knight* (2008) the Joker was unforgettably portrayed by the actor Heath Ledger. The Joker varies over the years from a relatively harmless though criminal buffoon to a figure of great power and sadistic humour, whose chief delight seems to be driving his adversaries into insanity or death through his bizarre, unpredictable 'tricks'. He uses such 'comic' weapons as razor-sharp playing cards, acid-squirting flowers, lethal 'joy buzzers' by which he kills with a handshake, and 'Joker venom', which causes his victims to die while uncontrollably laughing. He often seems to commit crime just for the fun of it, or because his inner perversity has run out of control.

Lately there has been quite a bit of discussion of the sociopath, or psychopath, in psychological literature. Was the Joker a 'comic' example? The sociopath is, at one extreme, the cold-blooded serial killer or murderer who appears to have no conscience, no ability to empathize with anyone else, who operates out of nothing but his own internal drives. Slightly tamed, she or he can also be the unscrupulous scam-artist or abusive spouse. Often individuals with this personality disorder can seem ordinary, even charming, on the surface, knowing well how to act normal enough to win the confidence of others in order to exploit them. Yet the sociopath's behaviour is characterized by deceitfulness, impulsiveness and lack of remorse for any cruelty to humans or animals. Lies and manipulation are the everyday tools, and crime, including rape and murder, their well-planned modes of predation when they calculate they can get by with it.

A certain number of people seem to be born sociopaths, exhibiting these characteristics from childhood on up, honing their skills to a fine point. No doubt a case could also be advanced that sociopaths can be made, perhaps by extreme initiations such as those that will be discussed in the next chapter. The Berserkers of ancient northern Europe, for example, will be shown to have become frenzied, conscienceless killers through initiations in which they assume the skin, and it was believed the spirit, of a ferocious beast such as wolf or bear.

The Joker clearly is a sociopath. Is the trickster also? One could certainly argue that he represents the mythology of such a psychopathic state. Coyote or Raven, like Hermes or Loki, were culture-bearers as well as destroyers, capable of doing favours as well as mean-spirited tricks. But what seems to be the case is that either way they acted not so much out of genuine good-will as out of their own inner feelings, perhaps not doing good as the sociopath might solely in order to win the confidence of some innocent victim, but certainly to please himself more than anyone else.

Two principal books on the sociopath, Robert Hare's *Without Conscience* and Martha Stout's *The Sociopath Next Door*, present differing views of the sociopath's inner life. Hare sees him or her as smug, self-satisfied, as it were always chuckling to himself, pleased with what he can get by with. Stout, on the other hand, believes the sociopath to feel inwardly empty, acting as he does to fill up an inner void; this chronic despair only gets worse with age.[68]

On the surface, the mythic Trickster would seem to be more like Hare's image. We see him brimming with clever ideas and plots, too many for his own good, and never tiring of his schemes even when they backfire. The Trickster's humour also works in his favour; we feel a common humanity with those who can laugh and joke, since we know that for ourselves humour is a good corrective to any pretension we may have to excessive grandeur; we are especially prone to laugh when the self-important slip and fall. We also feel for figures with whose situation we sympathize, like the slave John outsmarting Ole Massa, or Huckleberry Finn who keeps on going his own way whether in success or adversity.

Yet we ought also to remember the icon of the sad clown; outer humour can mask inner desperation. Indeed, the Trickster may mirror the general human condition more than we like to acknowledge. Even our good deeds not seldom come out of some inner impulse, or desire to impress or manipulate others, more than divine desire to accord with cosmic order, and we also may laugh on the outside while crying on the inside. In any case, the Trickster comes very close to the ultimate source of human evil, our own erratic nature.

Chapter 7

Traumatic Initiations

Birth and Death, and Everything In Between

Human life is a series of initiations.
    What is an initiation? Formally, the word means a beginning. Spiritually, it means a beginning in the sense of a new kind of life based on a change in the initiate. Initiation indicates a real change of consciousness, of awareness, of how one sees the world.
    Such changes are not merely intellectual. To truly make the individual a different person, they need to be reinforced by powerful sensory, emotional and physical stimuli that leave feeling and perhaps even bodily stigmata behind. One who has been ritually scarred or circumcised in an initiation does not easily forget the pain, and if she or he is ever inclined to do so, the bodily mark is there as a reminder of what happened. The initiate knows how to avoid, or perhaps regain, that pain or joy again through one's relationship to an irreversible initiation.
    Most important of all, the person is forever different from others outside the initiatory circle, and from whom he or she was before. One who has felt extreme fear, revulsion or divine ecstasy in the course of an initiation will continually retain the memory of that feeling somewhere in the background of consciousness, together with knowledge that only those of the same stamp are really like oneself deep within. If the rite was powerful enough, she or he is bonded above all else forever to those who shared the initiation, knowing only they can really understand. Only they will reliably act or dream in the same way as oneself. They are, it will often be said, brothers or sisters for life in a way even birth-siblings are not.

Initiations are of several types. First, there are those that are just part of life, and may be called natural initiations. Of these the greatest of all must be birth itself, our passage into the world. Ironically, birth must seem like a death, if one may so speak, to the foetus emerging from the womb. She or he must feel being pushed out of everything familiar, from out of a nine-months' world of enclosure, warmth, moisture, darkness and automatic nourishment. One is forced down a narrow canal, and then suddenly comes into a realm of blinding light and gigantic figures. No wonder newborn babies usually cry! Yet we on our side do not see it as death, but say, 'Hooray, a child is born into the world!'

Birth is a real initiation: a person come out into this light-and-dark world is forever different from the unborn. New senses, new kinds of awareness are suddenly opened up, though it takes time to get used to them, and the lessons of the natal process like any initiation were certainly reinforced by fear, pain and amazement. Although the pre-verbal child had no words for such states, undoubtedly they are very deeply etched on his or her pre-consciousness. All major subsequent initiations are in the end just repetitions of birth, or more precisely of what seems like a death followed by rebirth.

Birth is followed by other natural initiations: the great changes that come with puberty and adolescence; adulthood; becoming a parent oneself, especially being a woman herself giving birth; serious injury or sickness; entering old age and finally death at the other end of life, which can seem like the first part of an initiation of rebirth into another kind of life, and is so often regarded by religion.

All these keep to the model of dying to one kind of life and being reborn to another. The pubescent is dying to the world of childhood, and being born to that of a teenager and then an adult. Anyone who has had the experience of giving birth to a child, or who has undergone a major, life-threatening illness or injury, knows that one is not the same afterwards. Life is seen in a new way, as more precarious yet more precious than before. So also are relationships esteemed all the more deeply, and new kinds of kinship are forged with those who have shared the same edge-of-life experience.

Social Initiations

In most societies social initiations also occur, often parallel to natural initiations and often sanctified by religious services. Along with birth there come circumcision, baptism, blessing or presentation at a

Shinto shrine. Puberty rites include Christian confirmation and Jewish bar-mitzvah; entry into full adulthood can mean school-graduation and wedding ceremonies. And so it goes, up to the 'last rites' bestowed upon those about to undertake the final initiation. Often such rites as these are fairly perfunctory, though they attend major life-changes.

In some societies, particularly primal, the initiations of young men and women is often far more gruelling than these. In the area around Finschhafen, New Guinea, boys are taken from the village to the sound of whirring bullroarers, said to voice monstrous spirits of the dead, and the women – their mothers and sisters – weep to see them go, under the supposed illusion they will be eaten by a monster, called Balum (the same name as the bullroarer) and their loved ones will never see them again, unless they are redeemed by the offering of a pig. And they will not return – as boys. For they will come back reborn as men of the tribe, elaborately decorated with paint and mud, ready to feast and celebrate.[69]

During the three or four months away at a secret lodge in the forest said to be the belly of the ghostly monster, the boys would be painfully circumcised, eat the flesh of the sacrificed pigs, and be instructed in the lore of the tribe. In certain New Guinea tribes initiation includes the boys crawling through the legs of the men, in a manner powerfully imitative of birth.

Native American initiations were also memorable. A boy might spend days alone in the wilderness on a vision quest, waiting until he met his tutelary spirit, or wait for days in a sweat lodge, fasting, smoking the pipe, also waiting for spiritual contact. Other initiations involved pain. Perhaps the most excruciating of all was the four-day Okipa ordeal of the Mandan Sioux which included, after fasting, piercing skin and flesh with a saw-tooth-edged knife and inserting sharp sticks through the wounds, then suspending the initiates by leather thongs attached to these chest- or shoulder-piercing sticks, usually until the boy fainted. This ordeal was followed by cutting off the initiates' little fingers, and finally by their running around the compound with what strength they had left. The initiation was indeed a matter of death and rebirth, for it was alleged that those who emerged from this horrific rite remembered nothing of their previous lives.[70]

Initiations are also held for girls in many societies. Usually these are associated with the onset of menstruation. In Australia, the girl was taken to a sacred and secluded location, and her first menstrual blood was considered magically powerful. Afterwards she was brought back into the camp in a dancing, triumphant procession of women.[71]

Individual Initiations

Then we must recognize initiations which, while recognized to be of value by the society, are reserved for smaller groups of persons, or are even individual. These would first of all be initiations into such groups as fraternities and sororities, lodges of the Masonic type, spiritual orders lay or monastic, priesthoods. The initiatory ceremonies of largely secular groups like fraternities may be physically and emotionally demanding, as we shall see; so are those of some spiritual discipleships, such as Tantric Hinduism and esoteric Buddhist orders, for example Shugendo in Japan. But while Western spiritual group initiations or ordinations today are often serious and substantial, and may entail such supports as blindfolds and prostrations, they are usually not physically painful.

Socially-recognized but individual initiatory roles are exampled by such callings as those of the shaman or the Hindu sadhu or 'holy man'. Typically the shaman's initiation includes long periods alone in the wilderness, or in an isolated cave or cell, at which spiritual experiences interpreted as inner initiation take place. Certain Siberian shaman believed they were taken by a great bird of prey to the master shaman at the North Pole, the supreme initiator; or had their body taken apart and reassembled imbued with power; or were spiritually married to their female guiding spirit. Shamans among the Shuswap, a Salish tribe of British Columbia, was initiated by animals, who became his guardian spirits. The candidate would spend nights in the sweat lodge, until he dreamed the animal came to him and promised his help. The guardian-spirit animal gave him a song with which to call him; no one else was allowed to sing this song.[72]

Finally, the annals of mysticism and spirituality confirm that many persons of rich experience in these areas have gone through what amounts to inner initiations. They have fasted and struggled, endured physical and mental pain, have been tempted by demons or the equivalent, suffered the dark night of the soul, when it all seemed dust and ashes. Coming out on the other side, however, the initiate may enter into the unitive state, oneness with God or spiritual reality.

C. W. Leadbeater has written of what he terms the fourth initiation, explicitly compared to the crucifixion of Christ but now an inner experience, in uncompromising terms:

> It is one of the features of the fourth Initiation that the man** shall be left entirely alone. First he has to stand alone on the physical

plane; all his friends turn against him through some misunderstanding; it all comes right afterwards, but for the time the man is left with the feeling all the world is against him.

Perhaps that is not so great a trial, but there is another and inner side to it; for he has also to experience for a moment the condition called Avichi [a Buddhist term], which means 'the waveless, that which is without vibration.' The state of Avichi is not, as has been popularly supposed, some kind of hell, but is a condition in which the man stands absolutely alone in space, and feels cut off from all life . . . and it is without doubt the most ghastly experience that it is possible for any human to have. It is said to last only for a moment, but to those who have felt its supreme horror it seemed an eternity, for at that level time and space do not exist.[73]

The point is that all these initiations involve pain, which would seem to be evil, but the painful rite is for the purpose of initiation. One explanation of evil, then, is that it is necessary as means to higher good by supplying the ordeal for an initiation which strengthens and enlightens the initiate. The fear and circumcision agony undergone by the New Guinea boys made them into men; the shaman's ordeal gives him wisdom that can only be learned apart from others; Leadbeater explicitly viewed the fourth initiation as parallel to the crucifixion of Christ, which brought great good to the world. The ancient Christian martyr St Ignatius of Antioch, as he was being transported to Rome where he expected to be given to hungry beasts in the coliseum, wrote: 'May I find my joy in the beasts that have been made ready for me . . . let them all assail me, so long as I get to Jesus Christ . . . The pangs of new birth are upon me. Forgive me, brethren. Do nothing to prevent this new life.'[74]

Bear-shirted Beasts of Battle

But is the outcome of initiation always a higher good? That judgement, of course, requires perspectives which may not be shared by the participants. But some initiations have produced individuals moulded into groups that caused far more fear than joy. Take for example the Berserkers of ancient northern Europe. These were warrior bands under the patronage of Odin who, like the female Maenads of ancient Greece already mentioned, fought in a kind of ecstatic fury (called *wut*) and with animal ferocity. 'Berserker' probably means 'bear-shirted' (though 'bare-shirted', in the sense of without shield or armour, has also been suggested), which is as much as to say, identified with the spirit of a bear, or it seems in some cases of a wolf. In their fighting rapture, they made the sounds of the enraged beast, they grappled without mercy like one; for all intents and purposes the berserker *was* a bear or wolf.

Yet they were also sacred to Odin; it has even been suggested that they enacted a necessary counterbalance within society, 'representing the wild and fantastic in contrast with law and order',[75] perhaps like those 'ritual clowns' or the medieval 'boy bishops' who burlesqued the performances of solemn priests. In any case, they offered a recognized, and feared, power of their own.

Forming persons able to call up the demonic frenzy of *wut*, 'a mysterious, nonhuman, and irresistible force that his fighting effort and vigor summoned from the utmost depth of his being',[76] must have required serious initiation. The full scenario is not completely understood, and may not always have been identical. References in ancient sagas and histories make it clear that some candidates had to kill an enemy before he could cut his own hair or beard, or had to fight a bear to the death, or had to be able to fight unarmed. They may have entered a cave, and there dueled with no less than ten initiated berserkers. The culminating rite of passage into berserkerdom came when the candidate was ritually clothed in the skin of a bear or wolf, clearly an act of imparting to him the consciousness and quasi-magical soul of the beast of prey.[77]

Pollsmoor Prison, Cape Town

Here is the initiation from a very different time and place. A fascinating book by Jonny Steinberg, *The Number*, presents black prison gangs in contemporary South Africa through the eyes of an inmate of the vast Pollsmoor Prison in Cape Town. These gangs have a remarkable mythology and nomenclature, together with violent rituals and initiations. The three major gangs are known by numbers: the 26s, 27s and 28s.

They all originated from bands of outlaws in late nineteenth and early twentieth century colonial South Africa, made up of young men who had left their ancestral homelands but refused wage employment from the white bosses. The most famous was called the Ninevites, after the biblical Nineveh which rebelled against the Lord, even as the gang rebelled against the white government. The Ninevites were led by a charismatic and imaginative young Zulu named Nongoloza, who shaped them into a paramilitary organization, with ranks and imaginary uniforms. However, rather than operating simply as black Robin Hoods, the Ninevites robbed rich and poor, blacks and whites alike. They are remembered by Johannesburg's African population with a mixture of fear and awe. Stories are told, no doubt embroidered, of Nongoloza's exploits, his opulent base in an abandoned mine, and his magical powers – it was said the bullets of white policemen bounced off these Ninevites.

The Ninevites were finally crushed around 1910. But the legend of Nongoloza, like that of certain pirates famous for swagger and cruelty, lived on among South Africa's teeming and oppressed black proletariat. Prison gangs, based on a highly mythical version of the founder's career, tried to reproduce Nongozola's hierarchy, and they repeated his ideology: that he and his followers became bandits because whites were robbing them of their land and forcing them to work like slaves in the mines.

The odd number names of the prison gangs are said to be based on the membership numbers of groups of Nongozola's followers who left to go their own way. The 26s and 28s differ on versions of the myth, and also on such matters as the legitimacy of homosexual relations, always an issue in a men's prison; the conflict not seldom became violent in Pollsmoor. The 27s are said to have as their mission trying to maintain peace between the other two.

As for initiation, here is Steinberg's account of the 'ancient mores of initiation' imparted to a new recruit:

> You are meant to begin by committing an act of violence, you must spill blood, and when the warders beat you for your transgression, you must not cry out in pain. Once you have come back from solitary confinement, you are passed from one senior member to another, and slowly taught gang language – *sabela* – and aspects of the history of Nongoloza, the arcane rules of your position in the gang.[78]

Fraternity Gang Rape

An example from still another very different milieu, reported in Peggy Sandy's book, *Fraternity Gang Rape*, spotlights an American college fraternity which had gotten into very serious trouble because of episodes of 'gang rape' at its parties. Yet the same underlying motif, initiation into a bonding and a state of consciousness that makes acceptable what would be morally unacceptable on an individual basis, clearly obtains here as well. Initiation can lead one to do what otherwise one would not do, and if that thing is evil, then initiation is a source of evil.

The initiations of this fraternity were traumatic enough. An insider, identified as Sean, said, 'We felt that salvation is achieved through brotherhood, and nothing else (certainly not our individuality) mattered at all.' He confided that after an initiation the brethren shared stories and laughed about it, about how they had 'fallen apart', cried and acted 'foolishly', but that no longer mattered: 'We were laughing together about our common weakness as individuals, because we were building bonds that were transforming us into something larger and, hopefully, stronger.' The laughter was, he perceived, to put their separate selves at a distance. 'We were collectively celebrating the death of our individuality.' Sean mentioned the symbolism in the initiation of the sun rising over a coffin, indicating one's rebirth as a perfect spiritual self after the mortal self had 'died' by joining the society. Brethren in the fraternity, then, were survivors, survivors of the 'punishment' and death of one kind of being, now living as another, more powerful brotherhood self.

The other side was that now they had no moral code except the brotherhood's; the fraternity was able to create a private society in which they could see those outside its parameters as dark and terrified and, in a real sense, subhuman. As Sean again put it:

> Everyone and everything was open to ridicule, all people and all standards became vulnerable, because we had powerfully felt our own vulnerability [in the initiation]. That was our deepest kept secret, the thing that really separated us from the world outside: we knew how insignificant people can feel when they are really up against the wall – how insignificant we felt during initiation ... Our initiation experience and new knowledge constituted the deepest insight and a sacred revelation ... Now we could be masters of life ... we could toy with it and watch with amusement as everyone else staggered blindly through it.[79]

Ironically, in view of the fraternity's customary attitude towards women, as among those with whose lives they could 'toy' and whose vulnerabilities they could exploit, the central figure in the myth behind their draconian initiation is an 'astral goddess'. The initiates claim that the secrets of the brotherhood were first given to them by a Greek goddess, and that it is to her astral plane that they ascend in initiation. But it is not uncommon for males who vaunt superiority over 'real' women here on earth to profess devotion to a divine female figure.

In this, as in so many initiations, men who feel powerless alone, as youths, as prisoners, as students, seek bonding to a group which collectively is all-powerful, perhaps its power strengthened all the more by identity with an animal or divine source of superhuman power. But with this power they can work evil and well as good, and the temptation towards the former, for those whose feeling raised by the loss of self in initiation to a place beyond good and evil, is very great.

Chapter 8

The Hero's Dragon

The Happy Fault

Let us now consider more fully the notion that evil essentially exists so that it can be overcome – for the sake of the hero or saviour's triumph. In Christianity *o felix culpa* (O happy fault) is a theological tradition, affirming one can dare to regard the sin that has come into the world as fortunate, since it was the precondition, so far as we can say, requiring the incarnation and victorious resurrection of Jesus Christ, divine events greater in good than any sin is evil. Similar opinions can be found in Islam, as it calls the 'age of ignorance' a necessary precursor to the mission of Muhammad and the revelation of the glorious Qur'an.

In the Hebrew scriptures, Exodus tells us it was the Lord who hardened Pharaoh's heart as he refused to let the people of Israel go at Moses' request, so that when they finally left, to pass through the parted waters of the Dead Sea and make their way to lonely Mt Sinai and the Promised Land, the glory of God and the heroism of his agent, Moses, was all the greater. Indeed, the prophet Isaiah later has the Lord say, 'I form the light, and create darkness: I make peace, and create evil; I the Lord do all these things' (Is. 45: 7) – the 'strange work of God' (see Is. 28: 21) by which the overall plan of God is advanced.

In this context, the prophet was speaking of the captivity of Israel in Babylon, and of God's use of the benign Emperor Cyrus. That great Persian monarch, an instrument of God though not of the chosen Hebrew people, was called to free the Jewish captives so they could return to their land. Of this ruler the Lord says he will 'open before him the two leaved gates, and the gates shall not be shut' (Is. 45: 1), and then to the children of Israel, 'I will give thee the treasures of darkness, and hidden riches of secret places' (45: 3). Cyrus, though a hero, is clearly nonetheless meant to be only an actor in a tremendous drama, one so vast and deep that the greater part of it was undoubtedly beyond his comprehension, and that of most of the Jews of his time as well. Yet he plays his part, and at the end the full meaning of the story will surely be made clear, when 'the earth shall be full of the knowledge of the Lord, as the waters cover the sea' (Is. 11: 9).

Conventional hero myths are not as explicit about strange work, since as stories they do not give all the backstories, or for that matter all the final scenes before the curtain rings down. Yet from the dramatic point of view clearly the more evil the adversary, the more splendid the hero's victory.

His or her special role is evidenced in the way the hero is of mysterious and quasi-divine background: perhaps born of a virgin, perhaps in a hidden place such as a stable or cave, perhaps like Herakles conceived of a divine father and human mother. Typically there is then an adversary opposed to the marvellous child: King Herod against Jesus, Hera full of hatred for Herakles because he was a product of her husband Zeus' philandering, Moses concealed in the basket of reeds to save him from genocide against his people. In all this we see, first, the emergence of the hero out of powers or levels of reality greater than human; if human evil was not exactly there for the sake of the hero's ultimate victory, it evoked a cosmic or divine response greater than itself.

Hindu Deities and Demons

In its developed theological form, the great Hindu epic, the Ramayana, basically goes like this: Prince Rama, the epic's hero and the seventh avatar of Vishnu, grows up with his brothers in the palace of their earthly father, King Dasharatha. But at sixteen, Rama is called by the sage Vishvamitra to fight against the evil rakshasas or demons who have been defiling his sacrifices. The sage presents the young prince with divine weapons to use in that struggle, and the master of the demons was Ravana; only Rama, according to the sage, can defeat them.

As a young man the hero then wins the hand of Sita, the beautiful and virtuous daughter of another king, Janaka, by bending the great bow of the god Shiva. On his return from Janaka's court, Rama's father wishes to make him his heir, but instead is forced to exile him from court owing to an intrigue. Rama goes into the forest, accompanied by Sita and his faithful brother, Laksmana.

There, the evil demon Ravana abducts Sita and takes her to his palace in Lanka. This opens the heroic core of the story, Rama's quest for and rescue of Sita, his charming consort. In this venture Rama is assisted by Hanuman, the monkey-god, and his army. They build a bridge to Lanka. After many battles, Rama succeeds in killing Ravana, the purpose for which he was sent to earth as Vishnu's avatar. In the remainder of the story, Rama twice tests Sita to make sure she had remained faithful to him during her captivity in Ravana's castle. The hero then reigns over a paradisal kingdom for a thousand years and more before returning back to heaven.

Rama, as an avatar of Vishnu, is an embodiment of dharma, cosmic order and social righteousness, for in the Bhagavad Gita that same deity says:

> When goodness [dharma] grows weak,
> When evil increases,
> I make myself a body.
>
> In every age I come back
> To deliver the holy,
> To destroy the sin of the sinner,
> To establish righteousness [dharma].[80]

His adversary, the abductor of Sita, the demonic Ravana, however had acquired his almost-equal power not by nature or grace, but by the practice of tapas, austerities capable of generating great heat and with it power, until Brahma himself was forced to make him a master of the black arts stronger than any other deva or demon.

But when Rama finally smashed the iron heart of the demon-king with one of the mighty weapons given to him by Vishvamitra, it was to show the superiority of dharma, the divine order of the universe itself, over any self-centred and individual power however great. In this connection, we may note that Sita as well had a close connection with nature and its innate goodness.

We are told she was an incarnation of Bhudevi, the Earth Goddess and a consort of Vishnu, even as Rama was avatar of the god himself. The very name Sita means 'furrow', as in soil, so telling us again of the lovely young earth mother's affinity with smiling fields and teeming life. When she left the capital Ayodhya to share exile with Rama and

Lakshmana, in their distress elephants rejected their food and cows refused to suckle their calves, and even the sun and stars went dim. Nature again answered when Ravana kidnapped the princess, for she is also mistress of animals: the wind rose, birds and animals forgot their usual rounds to run in anger after the shadow of their beautiful beloved.[81] Sita is victim and yet, at the same time, in an almost passive way, all-powerful.

The active hero can also be feminine. (It can even be the case that both hero and adversary are feminine. Consider Dorothy in *The Wizard of Oz* struggling against the Wicked Witch of the West, or the goddess Athena giving Medusa snakes for hair as punishment for defiling her temple in an affair with Poseidon, a union which incidentally resulted in Medusa's giving birth to the winged horse Pegasus.)

Another Hindu example of a goddess-heroine is the battle of the divine Durga against Mahisha, the buffalo demon – considered also a deity in some sources. Durga is a form of the Shakti, or divine energy, of Shiva. Mahisha, like Ravana, had acquired great power through tapas or austerities, taking control of the three worlds and even dethroning Indra and sending the gods to Brahma begging for help. It was then that the gods enlisted the help of Shiva's shakti-consort or, in a variant, created the all-powerful woman anew for this heroic purpose, since lore said that only a female could defeat Mahisha. She is often portrayed as a fierce-looking female riding a lion and holding the spear with which she was finally to slay the demon.

Durga first tried to bewitch her adversary by coming to him as Kalaratri (dark night), a female of enchanting beauty. But, though fascinated by her, Mahisha nonetheless responded by approaching the goddess in giant form, as large as a mountain. But the shakti of Shiva became fire and reduced him to ashes. A battle of shape-shifting ensued, with the demon becoming a lion, a man and finally an elephant; successively Durga decapitated the lion, stabbed the man, and cut off the elephant's trunk. At the end, after he had become a buffalo again, Durga managed to pierce him with her trident; he reverted to his original form, a giant with a thousand weapon-bearing arms. But she threw him to the ground, shot with an arrow, and finally destroyed him.[82]

As the energy of Shiva, the deity representing the essence of the universe, Durga, like Rama, represents the superior power of that which is in accordance with the heart of nature as it is, over against powers acquired by effort, whether magic or yoga, for the sake of one's own glory. The hero's victory, then, is a demonstration of truth, but without an adversary, the display would not be meaningful or even possible. Durga needed Mahisha to show truth triumphant; the hero needs the monster.

The Knight, the Lady and the Dragon

The necessity of the foe in the hero's adventure can then be postulated as an interpretation of evil. The hero myth, as read by such modern writers as Joseph Campbell, is centred on an idea that undertaking the hero's journey, with its many trials and initiations, is itself a good which virtually justifies evil in order that evil may be overcome; evil is falsehood made to test the knight of faith.

The myth of the hero – defeating a dragon or monster – representing the destructive forces of the universe, including both the chaos before creation and the evil will of those plotting to devour and destroy thereafter, is extremely ancient. As we have seen, at the very beginning of civilization in Mesopotamia, the myth of Marduk had that god defeating Tiamat, a symbol of primordial chaos, to bring the world into order. Marduk represents storm, rain and fertility, but above all order, the right ordering of society.

It may be that a Christianized version of the same common Near Eastern tale is found in the well-known story of St George and the dragon. He was a soldier in Caesar's legions, but also, like many in the early years of the fourth century, a Christian. Travelling through an ancient land, George came upon a town sunk into the depths of despair. Inquiring, he found that it was plagued by a dragon who demanded the regular sacrifice of a maiden chosen by lot, and now chance had fallen upon the city's beautiful princess. Knowing what he had to do, George confronted the dragon, subdued him, and required as his only payment the citizens' willingness to be baptized into the faith of Christ, though some say he also married the princess. Not long after (and this may be the only historical part of the story), St George himself paid the supreme price for that faith, being martyred in 303 CE in Lydda, Palestine, after gruesome tortures.[83]

This story resonated throughout the middle ages, to the extent that St George became the patron of faraway England, and undoubtedly inspired such later mythopoeic heroes as such as the Red Cross Knight graphically fighting a dragon and winning a lady in Edmund Spenser's *The Faerie Queene* (1590s).

The hero-lady-monster tale may have had further antecedents in the Greek myth of Theseus, Ariadne and the Minotaur. The half-human, half-bull Minotaur was kept in a labyrinth by King Minos of Crete; this horror required the annual sacrifice of seven young men and seven maidens from Athens. Theseus, son of the king of Athens and already a hero, volunteered one year to go as part of the terrible delegation. Minos' daughter, Ariadne, fell in love with Theseus. When the Athenian prince entered the labyrinth, she gave him a length of thread he could follow to find his way out again. He killed the monster, offered him as a sacrifice to Poseidon, and using the thread made his way back to the doors of the maze. He then sailed away with Ariadne as his bride – though, inexplicably, he then seems to have forgotten about her and left her behind after a stop on the isle of Naxos.

Also in Greek mythology, it is significant that Herakles (Hercules), in each of his celebrated twelve labours, engaged his human cleverness to employ a different tactic in defeating each of his enemies, who were little more than one-dimensional brutes or predicaments. He slew the Nemean lion with his bare hands, defeated the nine-headed Hydra by burning its eight mortal heads and burying the ninth, cleansed the Augean stable by diverting the water of a river, killed the brazen clawed and beaked Stymphalion birds by frightening them with a rattle and then shooting them as they took off, and so it went.

Further East, in Japan, Susanoo rescued and married a lovely maiden who was to be offered to a gigantic snake with eight heads; he accomplished the task by setting out eight full, tempting bowls of *sake* (rice wine). When the serpent had drunk deeply of all of them with all his eight heads and fallen into a stupor, Susanoo was easily able to slice him into eighty pieces. And so it goes, right up to Luke Skywalker destroying the technological monster which was the Death Star.

In each case, it is first of all clear that the hero is conspicuously more human than the monstrous adversary. Marduk, though fiery, is closer to the human ideal with his passion for order than shapeless and stormy Tiamat. A dragon or minotaur not only looks less human than a knightly warrior, he is driven by only one appetite rather than the complexity of emotions, or the devotion to duty beyond self, which can animate the human. In *The Lord of the Rings*, it will be noted that the evil orcs, though occasionally individualized, are apparently all sufficiently ugly and mean-tempered to be virtually indistinguishable to their adversaries, whereas the nine companions in the destruction of the Ring are of different folk – elves, dwarves, hobbits, men and a wizard – and diverse personalities.

The Failed Hero

An aspect of the hero story that deserves attention, and which is particularly cogent to an understanding of evil, is the hero who seems about to triumph, or who actually does triumph, yet before the completion of the story she or he fails. Among the ranks of immensely influential modern mythologies the first feature-length animated film, Walt Disney's 1937 *Snow White*, surely holds prominent place. Yet in it the heroine of that name, after passing through the ordeal of a night journey through a terrifying wood, and after bestowing blessings not only material but also of love on the Seven Dwarfs, succumbs to the blandishments of her wicked stepmother disguised as an aged peddler-woman. Or Frodo who, in *The Lord of the Rings*, endures the tremendous ordeal of bearing the Ring to Mt Doom, where it can be destroyed, but who refuses to do so at the last minute – and the baneful object is annihilated unwittingly by the Ring-Bearer's pitiful rival, Gollum.

Or, turning to classical mythology, consider St George, who as we have just noted was martyred for his faith – though of course from the spiritual point of view this is also a victory – no more than a very few years after conquering the dragon. Or Jason, of the Golden Fleece, who as an old man was wont to go out to gaze at the remains of the ship *Argos*, once the vehicle of his heroic glory but now only a decaying hulk on the beach, until one day he was poignantly killed, according to one tale, by a flying piece of the wreck blown off in the wind.

From the point of view of mythology of evil, these stories and many others like them seem to be saying that, just as the hero of most such myths is not immune to defects of character, so the pervasiveness of evil in the world assures that no worldly victory of the hero is likely to be complete or indelible. Nor is it likely to be single-handed; Odysseus required the help of his son Telemachus, among others; Theseus of Ariadne; and Frodo, even more significantly, of one in the role of an enemy, yet he of whom Gandalf had earlier said, 'And he [Gollum] is bound up with the fate of the Ring. My heart tells me that he has some part to play yet, for good or ill, before the end.'[84]

Even if a story as we have it ends 'And they lived happily ever after', we rightly wonder what it is we are not being told, for we know human life is not always happy or unending. Only in moving beyond the circles of this world, and taking into account those heroes of another stamp whose triumphs resound in the cosmos as well as this planet, in heaven as well as on earth, do we find undiluted joy or eternal life.

The Hero as Saviour

Let us refer then to the hero's quest, and evil, in relation not only to warrior heroes, but also those who carried the heroic model onto battlefields of the spirit: the great religious founders, like the Buddha, Jesus and Muhammad; the innumerable saints and exemplars of all faiths. The broad overall pattern of their lives parallels the adventure of the warrior hero: call, time of trials, confrontation with the great adversary, victory and reward. But now the struggle is not so much flesh and blood warfare, but of inner strife against the powers of darkness.

Here, as an example, is the life-story of Buddha. According to the mythic account, Siddhartha Gautama Sakya (c. 560–480 BCE), called the Buddha or Enlightened One, was only the last and culminating incarnation in a very long pilgrimage leading through many, many lifetimes towards the ultimate awakening he attained in ancient India. He had made a vow before the Buddha of the world previous to ours unimaginable aeons ago, that however long it took, how many obstacles had to be overcome, he himself would reach buddhahood.

He then passed through countless lifetimes as a 'bodhisattva' or one becoming a buddha. Some of these lives are described in the Jataka or 'birth' tales popular throughout south-east Asia. In a good number of them the future Buddha took embodiment as an animal, but one always possessed of exceptional courage, prepared to sacrifice himself for the others of his herd or band; in this way he was developing the egolessness and compassion of an enlightened being.

Finally the bodhisattva was born into that life of which he said at birth: 'This is my last lifetime. In this life I will achieve what I have come to accomplish.' He was then raised as a prince; the king his father, having been told that his was a special infant who would become either a world emperor or world enlightened one, was just perceptive to realize that if the marvellous child saw anything of the suffering of the world he would be so moved by compassion he would not be content to rule over the earth from a throne, but would want to become a buddha, teacher of gods and men, and show humanity the way out of suffering. So the ruler made for his son a pleasure palace containing in its halls and spacious gardens nothing to displease, and a high wall all around to keep out any sight of ill.

But the prince finally became curious what lay beyond those walls, from which his eyes had been thus far shielded. Riding into town in his chariot he caught sight of an aged man, a dying man, a corpse, and finally a monk with his staff and begging bowl. The youth now realized he could live for nothing but to understand what he had seen, and to learn how he and others could keep peace of mind in the face of old age, sickness, and death. He followed the example of the monk and set out on his own quest.

He tried several spiritual paths and teachings, but found them unsatisfactory. Then the evening came when he knew the time had come, and he would find out for himself. The royal scion turned monk seated himself under a great tree, and swore by the earth itself he would not stir from that spot till he had attained full and perfect enlightenment. In the early hours of the night an old demon or god called Mara, realizing that if this human reached Buddhahood he would be greater than any god, tried to dissuade him from his path, sending storm, sensual allurements, and finally spiritual temptation against him. But the Buddha rejected the old one with an upraised hand. Eventually Mara departed, and the Buddha sank into deeper and deeper trance. When the Morning Star appeared he attained full enlightenment. His mind became horizonless, one with the cosmos, able to penetrate infinite past and future. Above all he dwelt in the utter peace of Nirvana, since when one is one with all being, naught there is to fear.

That night of nights the Buddha also received the Four Noble Truths. He grasped that suffering pervades all of life, that suffering is caused by desires and their attachments; there can be an end to desires, and the way to that end is the Eightfold Path: right views, intentions, speech, conduct, livelihood, effort, mindfulness, all culminating in right concentration or meditation. We suffer, in other words, because we focus on particulars, missing the whole; moreover the particular, including attachment to our own particular lives, is always changing, continually coming into being and going out of being; only in the whole found in the depths of the meditative mind is there permanence.

Was the enlightenment he grasped something the Buddha attained alone, or was it a manifestation of a deep Reality that is everywhere, in all of us, only not seen because of our blinkered minds? This question has long been debated in Buddhist circles, but surely one can say that, just as the procession of ever-changing particulars has neither beginning nor end, so has the possibility of breaking through them to permanence and peace always been at hand for those able to seize it. Indeed, the permanent must be the substratum of the changing, like the timeless sea still and deep even as surface waves rise and fall.

The Buddha then, no less than the dragon-questing knight, is a hero for whom the enemy lives and breathes only to be overcome. But for this *jina* or conqueror the foe is no dragon except the dragon of ignorance, and the canker-worm of suffering we bring upon ourselves by seeing only baffling particulars out there and within ourselves. These illusions exist so as to be overcome by perseverance through the many lifetimes and many vicissitudes of a bodhisattva becoming a Buddha.

Miracle and Image

The Russian student of myth Aleksei Fyodorovich Losev (1893–1988) was long little known because of persecution during the Stalinist period, but is now attracting world attention for the philosophical profundity of his mythological thought, influenced though it was by Hegel and Schelling. Losev conceived of myth as dialectical, meaning that in mythic stories an entity is understood through its relationships, and most fundamentally of all, by what it is not. Such a clear-cut definition, setting a mythic figure in context yet also individualized, allows each entity – god, hero, ordinary human in interaction with them – to emerge as a clear *eidos* or image.

The need for self-definition is the fundamental problem of conscious personhood, our continual human condition, too. We need to know who we are and who we are not, as a person. In the dialectics of myth the issues of personhood are concrete, even as is our own personal experience. Identity is not a theoretical exercise based on probabilities like science. In myth the universe is alive, and puts consciousness at the centre. The hero contends not with bare natural forces or hard matter, but with gods of sun and moon, spirits good and bad, and living forests.

The Hegelian-type larger cosmogonic dialectic Losev saw underlying all 'real' mythology bespeaks the same *eidos* of individual/divine personhood set in its immense context: there is (1) a 'primordial luminous being', or simply primordial essence, (2) creation of the gods, world, humans, and then the historical process and (3) the primordial essence reaches 'self-consciousness of itself in other-being'.[85]

Another interesting idea of Losev's is that of what he called 'miracle' in myth. This notion, also inspired by Schelling, does not mean miracle in the usual supernatural sense, but 'breakthrough' moments of complete fulfilment of self as a process, like the victory of the hero or the creation of a world. Undoubtedly we have all had such moments of complete joy, love, success and fulfilment. Then one may be overwhelmed by feelings of magic, miracle, grace, well portrayed in the unambiguous triumphs and climaxes of myth.[86] Those there may be who disdain as 'escapist' finding love and joy in myth, but for Losev myth is a model against which to set the world, the map which can help us find real treasure.

These brief insights from Losev's complex and densely-packed work should make clear that, for him, myth spells dialectic consummation, light at the end of a long tunnel – divine self-consciousness, the 'miracle' of self-fulfilment – which on the human plane might best be imaged in the victory of the hero. But such a dialectical or process victory necessitates an adversary to be defeated. In sum, then, from the point of view of myth, evil has its inevitable role, and can be understood as the hero's dragon.

Chapter 9

Evil under Analysis

Evil as Story

What do these tales tell us about evil? First of all, perhaps they tell us more about the human condition than of evil in the abstract. They put evil in the context of human situations of extremity. Evil is not just a problem; it is a *human* problem, perhaps *the* human problem. Paul Ricoeur spoke of myth as that which lies before or beneath the philosophies: 'Behind speculation, and beneath gnosis and anti-gnostic constructions, we find *myths*.'[87]

To 'interpret' the myth in a language which, for the interpreter, seems more sophisticated than story is not so much an act of final rendition as of translation, changing the tale from a story of gods or primal people to one of social function or psychology. Nonetheless, it is important, for as we have seen, according to Claude Lévi-Strauss a myth is found in all its variants. Let us then look at myths of evil in light of a few of these interpretations. They are based on the theories of myth-interpretation presented in my book, *Myth: Key Concepts in Religion*.

The theories are here divided into four types: Euhemeric, Enlightenment, Romantic and Pedagogical. Examples of all four can be found in most periods, from antiquity on up: whenever someone looks at a myth, not just as a good story or as 'what all of us around here believe', but from an analytic point of view, some kind of theory or outside framework for understanding is operative. The four types seem to me to reflect not only perceptions in a formal sense, but also deep-seated attitudes or ways of thinking on the part of their proponents.

Euhemerism

Euhemeric theories of myth are named after the Greek writer Euhemeros (c. 330–260 BCE), who claimed, like many later rationalistic writers, that myths are not literally true, but are based on historical figures and events that, in the retelling, were more and more exaggerated until great kings became gods, and great spiritual leaders became saviours and divine incarnations. Euhemeros was in the employ of Alexander the Great, and he may well have had opportunity to observe the beginning of that process. For the Macedonian conqueror soon enough became the hero of legends told across Europe and Asia.

He was said to be actually the son of Nectanebo II, last native pharaoh of Egypt, who being also a magician took the form of a serpent and impregnated Olympias, Alexander's mother; the victorious Greek was thus assured the pharaohs' divine descent and legitimacy as ruler of Egypt, which he subsequently conquered, as well as acquiring the semi-virgin birth of many heroes. Striding towards the ends of the earth, he invented a flying machine and a diving bell, as well as discovering a fountain of youth and becoming 'King of the World'.[88] There are even accounts that the invincible champion reached the gates of Paradise.[89]

Named or not, the Euhemeric approach has had a long history. Sceptical Roman writers used it to naturalize and explain away myths that seemed unbelievable, as did medieval Christian writers to neutralize stories of pagan gods, both Greco-Roman and Nordic, who could not be real deities by the light of Christian faith. Still later, critical commentators on the Bible and other sacred texts, as well as on countless holy legends and credulous accounts, have endeavoured to humanize holy persons and search out the roots of stories, to show how men and women became myth; note the title of Albert Schweitzer's classic book, *The Quest of the Historical Jesus* (Eng. transl. 1910).

One figure of particular interest is Sir James Frazer (1854–1941), author of that many-volume work, *The Golden Bough*, which traced myth and religion back to the periodic ritual killing of priest or sacred king, whose death imparted fertilizing life to the land. Frazer began his study with the dramatic account of a sacred grove of Diana at Nemi, near ancient Rome. An ancient legend, we are told, declared that if a runaway slave managed to pull down a bough from a particular golden tree, he had the right to slay the priest of that shrine if he could, and succeed him as 'King of the Wood'. We are then off into many pages and finally volumes of lore of this kind, in which a sacred murder is presented as the ultimate background of myth and ritual around the world.

An example like this should make it clear that the relation of Euhemerism to the mythology of evil is quite ambivalent. On the one hand, by showing the gods are but humans writ large, the theory leaves the gods no better than humans: Zeus with his many adulteries and his violence, Diana the huntress whose priest is proclaimed by assassination, were perhaps ancient tyrants or sorceresses of like proclivities in Euhemerist eyes. At the same time, by demystifying all-too-human deities, the theory voids the need to believe in or emulate them, preparing the way for a more humane society or religion.

Functionalism

The Functionalist view of myth, expressed mainly by the anthropologist Bronislaw Malinowski (1884–1942), is based on the idea that a myth, or ritual practice, can only be understood in light of its function in a particular society; comparisons with other societies are of little value. According to Malinowski, in primal culture myth fuelled the functions of expressing and codifying the worldview and the moral values that went with it. '[T]he myth conveys much more . . . than is contained in the mere story . . .' but also within it lie 'the traditional foundations of social organization', and these the person within a society learns not only from the story, but from knowing the story within the context of tribal society. '[I]t is the context of social life, it is the gradual realization by the native of how everything which he is told to do has its precedent and pattern in bygone times, which brings home to him the full account and the full meaning of his myths of origin.'[90]

Myth maintains the social system by justifying its key components, especially through 'charter' myths that present the origins of institutions. For it is always assumed that if we know where something came from we know what it is and why it must be done as it is done. Such myths tell why the king is of a certain lineage, certain taboos are observed, or women and perhaps castes have their often-subordinate places in the social order. But while these myths may rationalize practices that might otherwise have been considered evil, the problem of evil is not entirely solved.

For example, a king in ancient northern Europe may have considered Berserkers necessary as crack troops in his wars, or as a way to give potential troublemakers useful roles. But questions remain, as they do regarding many initiations today, about the dulling of moral sensitivity in Berserker rites, and the gratuitous violence these human animals enacted. Designating certain persons as 'witches' enables a society to draw boundaries and determine who has standing as a legitimate member of the social order, and who is excluded.

But ideal justice may still not be served. Is it truly right to outcast persons on the basis of defects of mind or body that make them seem 'odd' to 'normal' folks? And the functionalist myth has no backstory to tell why ours is this kind of a world, where evil has residence, in the first place.

Structuralism

This approach, identified with Claude Lévi-Strauss (1908–) and others, views myth as meeting the more universal task of reconciling opposites: male and female, day and night, us and them. Lévi-Strauss himself liked to compare myth to music, with its high and low notes making an overall harmony. The Trickster figure, for example, brings together human and animal, rational and wilful, daring and yet often comically self-defeating. The Babylonian creation myth, as we have seen, set land and sea, salt and fresh waters, chaos and structure over against each other, but in the end reconciled them to form a livable world. Scholars in the structuralist tradition like Mircea Eliade (1907–86) have proceeded to contrast sacred and profane space and time (the temple versus the ordinary world; the time of festival and rite versus everyday time), or the *illud tempus*, 'that time', the mythic time when the gods were powerful, and today. A sacred site is often marked by a sacred tree or mountain as *axis mundi*, pivot of the world, or sacred time by special gestures or even language.

Yet, so far as the problem of evil is concerned, structuralism does not so much solve as rationalize the issue, by endeavouring to make the irrational integrated parts of a rational creation. In the end, though there may be alleviation through wisdom, the pain is still there.

Psychoanalysis

According to Sigmund Freud (1856–1939) and his psychoanalysis, myths are the collective dreams of humanity, and dreams are windows into the pressure cooker of internal psychological dynamics. This particular cooker is far more universal in its contents and dynamics than it is culture-specific. For what all of us, from Eskimos to Ecuadoreans, had in common, especially as children, is in the end far more consequential than differences.

For did we not all have parents, and sexual drives veiled or otherwise? Did we not all grow up from the child's perspective, when father and mother seemed like gigantic omnipotent beings, into adolescence and adulthood, when other angles of vision and other energies drove our world? Yet the former things were never lost, remaining lodged in the deep recesses of consciousness.

That place is the gate of dreams, and it is hardly a wonder that so many myths, like the Greek creation account in Hesiod, present often-unpleasant tales (fantasies?) of incest, parricide, sibling rivalry and the omnipotent child.

Freud insisted that the drives which propel the libido or 'pleasure principle' that seeks fulfilment, like the social inhibitions that frustrate it, are biological at root. They are grounded in the human animal's need to mate, reproduce, nurture and be nurtured. What Freud considered being a universal taboo against incest clearly originated in these needs, as did what he called the Oedipus complex, significantly named after a myth: the guilty desire of the child to conjoin with the parent of the opposite sex and supplant the parent of the same gender.[91]

By way of further example, Dan Merkur considers a widespread Native American myth called 'The Release of the Wild Animals'. It relates that in the beginning all game animals, and in some versions botanical foodstuffs – vegetables, fruit and nuts – as well, are all confined in one small, secret place. The culture-hero finds that place and releases the sources of food for the benefit of human beings, whether by victory over the secret's shadowy guardian, or at the cost of his own punishment, like Prometheus bringing fire.

Merkur speculates that, from the Freudian perspective, this myth could be interpreted as a symbolic representation of a boy's battle with his father over access to his mother, whose womb and breasts were the ultimate, original sources of food. Whether he is victorious or punished, or in some sense both, the Oedipus myth is clearly reflected, as is the biological source of the suffering and evil this struggle entails.[92]

Or, if we want to bring Oedipus up to date in contemporary myth, consider Darth Vader ('Death Father?') in *Star Wars*, the father against whom his own son Luke Skywalker had to struggle almost to the death, in order to liberate the galaxy and bring it back to the nurturing fecundity and beauty it had in the days of his mother, who died giving birth to him and his sister Princess Leia.

Mythological evil, in Freud's materialistic world, is therefore biological at its source. Myth limns, perhaps in dreamlike symbol, the seething sexual and murderous appetites just beneath the surface of consciousness that can never be fulfilled outwardly, unless at the cost of great destructiveness both to ourselves and others; and myth no less expresses the bitterness that wells up behind the barriers civilization must set up against childish rampage and orgy.

What is repressed in broad daylight can still live on in dream and myth, and in the great tides of desire, guilt, fear and frustration that wash through those lower-level streams of consciousness. Being biological in a materialistic world, they are beyond, or beneath, good and evil. Judgement about righteousness rests rather with society, in its collective decisions on how to deal with them. The upshot usually leaves the society's citizens conformist, vaguely discontented yet functional; occasionally the repressed energies may explode in rage or war.[93]

Analytic Psychology

Carl Gustav Jung (1875–1961) was a disciple of Freud who broke with him, fundamentally on the grounds that the older man's primary association of unconscious drives with sexual energy was too restrictive. Jung's analytic psychology, as he called it, looked at life less in terms of its infantile commencement, than in its goal: what he called individuation, complete and independent adult humanness.

To get individuated we must balance off several different ambitious aspects of the psychic person. In myth, dream, fantasy and religion these aspects may be articulated as what are called archetypes, figures representing various personality ideals: the Great Mother, the Wise Old Man, the Hero, the Maiden, the Shadow, etc. The Great Mother, for example, may be expressed in an idealized mental picture of one's own mother, or some other motherly image, or in a dream image, or in such religio-mythical forms as Isis, the Chinese Queen Mother of the West, Parvati, the Virgin Mary.[94]

Evil, of course, is made manifest in the Shadow archetype. It is said to consist of parts of the mind containing repressed undesired animal instincts, weaknesses or anxiety over inferiority. The Shadow is irrational and can easily project itself onto someone else, so that one sees in another an unacknowledged failing of one's own: members of one race 'projecting' their turbulent but unwelcome aggressive or sexual fantasies onto another race.

The Shadow no less takes shape in dreams and imaginings, frequently as a fearful monster or personal adversary. But one may also interact with the Shadow persona, or even identify with it – because it is really within oneself. Jungian therapists say it is necessary to recognize one's Shadow and come to terms with it, learning to use its energies in positive ways.

The Jungian source of evil, then, may ultimately lie in our biological nature, but it is conceptualized in terms of a complex process of individuation, in which it may be that not all parts of the psyche develop together at the same rate, or fit together easily. In particular, those aspects of the self that are at the opposite of one's strongest features may be neglected, and so take undesirable Shadow qualities. A highly intellectual person disdains others he considers too emotional; but that intellectual may actually be pursued in dreams by a black fog that seems to be all irrational feeling. A feeling-type individual may talk contempt for those she considers to 'live just in their heads', and get angry or depressed at difficulty in dealing with abstractions like numbers. This, and much more, could be the seeds of myth, as well as calls to cultivate a more balanced psychic life.

In the last analysis analytic psychology, like other theories of myth and evil, can chart insightfully the eddies and currents of the river of thought, but cannot trace them entirely back to the wellspring. Evil remains the mystery of iniquity, the irrational in a reasonable world. It was the great bugbear of enlightenment thought, even when science turned reason's all-seeing eye to angles as odd as those of psychoanalysis where, beneath the surface of the enlightened mind, its doctors saw reason grew very dim indeed, and instead a simmering stew of monsters and phantoms.

Romanticism

Another modern view of myth virtually rejoiced in the non-rational. By the late eighteenth century, as the romantic mood began the supplant the enlightenment, feeling and imagination looked more valid than reason as keys to that which lies at or beyond the fringes of human consciousness. This perception applied supremely to the understanding of myth, for myth has ever suggested that profound significance awaits us like a buried treasure, beneath the drab surface of old stories' oft-naive or disconcerting narratives.

For romantic thinkers, mythic tales offered at least a sense of the remote distant and past, bound to evoke feelings of wonder and challenge imagination. In an era of emergent nationalism, they also offered an aperture into the spirit of the people who told them, and the meaning of that spirit in their days of pristine, primordial beginning. Back then, men and women were held to be strong and direct, humans as they were meant to be before the corrupting influence of too much civilization.

This was the doctrine of Johann Gottfried Herder (1744–1803), who emphasized the way the myths of his native Germany were shaped by that land's language and natural environment.[95] Against enlightenment *philosophes* like Bayle and Voltaire he insisted myths were not just lies concocted by deceitful priests to gain power over the credulous people; the shamans of central Asia, for example, merely expressed in the form of myth natural hopes and dreams, even as does great poetry.[96]

The philosopher Friedrich Wilhelm von Schelling (1775–1854) saw myth-making as the profoundest of all human arts, for in myth the secrets of original human nature are concealed, to be released by philosophy combined with mythology; abstract language is only 'faded mythology', for since our lives are stories, myths tell their meaning best, and the various mythologies are like stained-glass windows that refract the ultimate 'potencies' of the divine essence in different guises.[97]

The recent writer most in the romantic tradition is undoubtedly Joseph Campbell (1904–87). Though widely learned in world mythological traditions, and able to recount their stories eloquently, Campbell seemed above all interested in what myth had to tell humans today about life. As one acute critic of Campbell, Robert Segal, put it, Campbell 'is oddly not much interested in myth – as myth. He is much more interested in human nature, which he simply finds revealed in myth.'[98]

As we have seen, Campbell's great interest was in the hero's journey, in his view the archetype of a productive human life. Like all myth, the hero's story had power to place a person's life in the largest possible context, the infinite universe itself, 'so that he recognizes that he participates in it, since the mystery of being is the mystery of his own being as well.'[99]

Romantic nationalism, as has been suggested, was concerned with the mystery of national identity as well. Heroic mythic narratives were an important part of exploration into that mystery, for a nation's heroes presumably embodied its innermost spirit and highest ideals: thus the *Kalevala* in Finland, in France tales of Charlemagne and Roland, in Germany the stories from the medieval *Nibelungenlied* best known through the mighty operas of Richard Wagner, in England the rediscovery of King Arthur and his knights, retold in Victorian idiom by Tennyson in his *Idylls of the King*.[100]

As with other examples of mythic theory in respect to the problem of evil, romanticism presents a two-edged sword. One blade faces outward, the other inward against the theory itself. On one hand, myths viewed through the romantic lens, above all heroic and national myths, almost inevitably involve conflict and therefore 'good guys' versus their opponents. The myth can provide all too easy vehicles for demonizing enemies, who may well be simply persons of another nation, race or religion. Romantic exaltation of feeling and imagination facilitates this process, insofar as it supersedes careful rational analysis of a situation with the sort of broad characterizations most satisfying to the emotions. To be sure, romantic nationalism has sometimes fuelled worthwhile drives for independence and reform ('make the nation worthy of its heroes'), and inspired great art, but the dangers should be obvious.

Turned against itself, romantic theory driven by conflict needs evil and provides no answer to the problem of evil except that suggested in our previous chapter on the hero and his dragon; that heroism – and with it virtually mystical feelings of exultation and victory – is the supreme goal of human life, and therefore evil is necessary as the adversary over which one is to win. Does this mean that romanticism itself is evil? No answer to that query is given here, for myth has no ultimate backstory; beyond the conquering hero it cannot go.

Pedagogical Theory

Using myths as philosophical teaching devices was most famously propounded by Plato.[101] Consider his myth of the cave in *The Republic*. In this remarkable cave people are bound in such a way that they can face in only one direction. Looking this way, they are unable to see Reality, but only the shadows of Reality cast on a wall in front of them.

One rebel manages to get behind the scenes, where he detects the fires casting the shadows, the parading objects whose shades the prisoners take for 'reality', and finally the unimagined light of day itself as he escapes from the cave altogether. But upon his return to tell *that* story he is regarded not as liberator but as mad.

It might be added that, in *The Republic*, Plato wanted to exclude, or at least severely censor, poets and myth-makers in his ideal city. In his eyes they were no better than the Sophists, teachers of rhetoric prepared to argue any side of a question; both the poets and the Sophists used words, *logoi*, to mean whatever they wanted them to mean at the moment, as though all was in flux, as Heracleitus had earlier claimed, and neither language nor the ideas behind it had any permanent meaning.

Moreover, poetry and myth dealt with undesirable topics. Plato would, for example, have suppressed Odysseus' journey to the Underworld in the Odyssey because of the negative impression of death it gave, for he wanted the citizens of his utopia to be fearless in the face of death. Likewise Hesiod's creation myth, with its promiscuously quarrelling and copulating gods, must be excised, for in the Republic sex was strictly controlled to produce the best possible children, who were raised not in families but by the community as a whole. His perfect state was not a democracy, but a meritocracy, rule by the best, guided by supreme wisdom.

How far Plato meant his blueprint to be taken absolutely seriously, and how much he intended only to be provocative and get some good arguments going, is still intensely debated. It is clear, however, that the great philosopher sets *logos*, word (and much more), over against *muthos*, myth. *Logos* was really idea and knowledge in the philosophical, scientific and mathematical sense; education in the Republic emphasized math. *Muthos* was story as fabulous accounts based on feeling, imagination or unfounded opinion, all of which Plato greatly distrusted. Today no less than in ancient Athens these two sides stand over against each other. Do we trust science or religion, mathematical or mythical models, to give us the profoundest picture of what the universe, and human life in it, is all about?

And yet it can be said that Plato was himself a poet and myth-maker, and that his characteristic use of dialogue as a means of expounding philosophical notions suggests that the significant realization of truth is a process, not an absolute. Towards this end several styles of language can be employed, though perhaps ultimately Plato (through his chief interlocutor, Socrates) would contend that his poetry, myths and conversations can point towards the clarification of eternal realities, as well as their mystification.

In the middle ages, many ancient myths, especially as recited by the Latin poet Ovid, were told with edifying morals in mind; countless sermons employ myth-type stories from sacred scriptures the same way.

However, because pedagogical myth seems rather derivative and contrived, it is not taken seriously today as a theory of primordial, preliterate myth. It may combat evil through moralizing, but although many people like a good story, not all are converted by a moralistic tag-line at the end; the story must do more if it is really going to change hearts and minds.

When a story grips us, whether it is heard, watched on a screen, or read, what does that mean exactly? Not necessarily that it is true in some objective sense, or that we have invoked a 'willing suspension of disbelief', but that the receiver is feeling and imagining along with the tale. The narrative is activating those areas of mind where the images associated with emotion arise, to form the seeds of ongoing attitudes and responses.

To put the matter more simply, we feel anger at figures in the story that made us angry, we feel exultation at a happy outcome, we share in the point-of-view character's fears and frustrations, her loves and loathings. These impulses are bound to leave a residue, and to that extent we are changed by the story.

New programs have been made accessible to our mental computers; new pictures have been added to our inner gallery of ways to image the world. If these fancies add to the evil of which we are capable, if they add gluttonous or sadistic fantasies to our inner trove, the story is in the evil camp at least for us. If new images show us better how to learn and do good, and make us want to explore that path, the moral may be achieved not as a maxim, but through the story itself.

Following this pattern, we will next look at how myth can provide a way back out of the toils of evil.

Part II

The Road Back: Curing Evil

Chapter 10

Laughter and Wisdom

In and Out of the Trap

In this concluding section of our study of the mythology of evil, we will see that myth not only shows how we and our world have gotten enmeshed in evil, but can also show us the way out of the trap. Again, myth will not offer a complete explanation, because myth can only start in the middle of a story that has no real beginning. But the myth-explanation is a significant one because it puts the struggle in and out of evil into the perspective of the universe as humanly significant.

Let us think for a moment about ancient Greek myth and philosophy. It could be, and has been, argued that Hesiod's myths of creation, in which as we have seen evil seems to have been built into the fabric of a universe of struggling gods, was only fable or poetry. But, sceptics of such tales will say, the beginnings of Greek philosophy and science, usually assigned to Thales (fl. c. 580 BCE), marked a new venture founded on empirical observation interpreted by reason. Thales taught the basic principle of the cosmos was water. As wrong as Thales may have been about water, this theory, together with other discoveries in mathematics, astronomy and physics attributed to him, moved human thought from myth to the scientific use of observation and reason to get at the real nature of the universe – and to discover that nature is not rumbustious fighting and lovemaking gods, but simple elemental substances and natural law.

But what about the mind behind the eye making these empirical observations and deductive reasonings? Is its consciousness also part of the universe, part of a larger field of consciousness in which Thales participated, or was mind strictly confined to Thales' head, his loftiest ideas only the secretions of a brain that had evolved out of sea-water and like substances in a purely materialistic way? If the latter holds true, then the gods are best forgotten, except as figments of poetry. But if mind is more than brain, then the squabbling deities can at least be taken to represent something tremendously important, that consciousness is behind the universe as well as emergent in animals and human beings, coming first as well as last, making the universe as humanly significant on the level of mind as well as of matter.

Hesiod at the outset of his *Theogony* first invoked the Muses, sources of inspiration, suggesting wisdom comes from a consciousness-field larger than an individual head. A very fundamental issue – perhaps *the* fundamental issue – between religion, including mythology, and the sort of empirical, rationalistic philosophy and science that began with Thales, is simply the question of whether consciousness is strictly confined to humans and other sentient biological beings. Is the rest of nature from sea to stars no more than the unconscious matter it appears to be in our eyes? Or are other planes and fields of consciousness, mostly invisible, out there as well: gods, angels, demons, perhaps a universal mind that underlies the seemingly mindless cosmos that meets our five senses?

Traditional myth generally evokes consciousnesses mighty and minuscule behind the 'dead' surfaces of nature, thereby making the universe humanly significant and showing that what it does can be understood, and engaged, through passions known to us by means of our own minds: the gods are angry, pleased, persuadable and indifferent. Thus the countering of evil can start as a matter of mind: say a sense of humour.

Salvation by Laughter

Do those myths which present the cause of evil in a humorous light, as do many stories of the Trickster or the trivial 'accident' or misunderstanding that sets wickedness loose in the world, suggest that the best antidote to evil is accepting it in the same spirit? We do well to go along with the joke, they seem to say, even when it is on us; at least then we are less likely to fall into the worse end of tragedy.

We have already noted the dark, perhaps ironic humour of those myths of creation which fix the whole future race in the grip of evil and death because of a single bad choice, like the Celebesians taking the banana instead of the stone, or because of the presumption and folly of a single creature like the Limba toad who thought he could carry the medicine of immortality to humankind better than the serpent. One can well imagine a gifted storyteller playing up these narratives to great comic effect. Nonetheless the fact remains they show the line between life and death, good and evil destiny for our kindred, to be fine indeed. It looks like it could have easily gone either way. So it was with those disastrous misjudgements on the part of a Trickster, when his 'jokes' or impetuousness or greed got the better of him, and Coyote lost us the light of the sun-in-a-box, or Loki the life of a beautiful god.

In the not dissimilar Garden of Eden story, the general response has been to bemoan the failure of our first parents. But not a few primal peoples seem to have felt that, if there is nothing we can do about it now, why not laugh instead of weep? Humour basically comes from perceiving the incongruity between what ought to be, or is expected to be, and what is – and at the same time laughter, because it feels good, makes it possible for us to live with, even enjoy, the disconnection. If it were not there, what would there be to laugh about?

One of the greatest laughter myths of all is Japanese. At the beginning of this story, Amaterasu, the beautiful goddess associated with the sun, dwelt with her maidens on the High Plain of Heaven, where she had broad and narrow rice fields, and where she and her attendants did weaving and celebrated the ancient harvest festival.

But her brother Susanoo, the storm-god, was angered by his placement on earth while his lovely sister rode the skies. He determined to visit her, at first in a friendly way. But soon they quarrelled, and Susanoo's violent temper went out of control. He rampaged through the rice fields, ruining the crops. He defiled the room where the harvest festival held by rudely defecating in it. Finally, he polluted the heavenly weaving-hall by throwing the backward-skinned (against nature) body of a pony onto the middle of the floor. Amaterasu, offended and frightened beyond measure, retreated into the rock-cave of heaven, depriving the earth of light.

By now all the gods were worried about these unnatural happenings in heaven. They assembled amid the gathering darkness in the River of Heaven (the Milky Way) to discuss the matter. Finally, as no resolution seemed to be at hand, a goddess named Ama-no-Uzume got up and, standing on an upturned tub, began to do a humorous ribald dance – the incongruity of a goddess acting in a clownish way. The forgathered deities burst into raucous laughter, the peals of their divine merriment ringing through the cosmos.

Amaterasu sulking in her dim cave heard the roar of their resounding mirth. Forgetting her fear, she stuck her head out to see what was going on. As soon as the goddess' brilliance was visible, a god held a sacred mirror before her face, and began backing up. Fascinated by her own beauty, Amaterasu followed him and the mirror out of the cave, and light returned to the world.

It may be noted that laughter is still a part of some Japanese festivals. At the best-known shrine of Susanoo in Japan, the Yasaka Shrine in Kyoto, on New Year's Eve worshippers stand in two groups facing each other and shout loud abuse at each other, like Amaterasu and Susanoo but in a humorous vein, until listeners are holding their sides with laughter.[102]

By setting our minds on the right coordinates, it is possible to find the way out of the morass of evil. On this journey, laughter may well be the best medicine. But while you are laughing, you can also be travelling towards the world before the joke. That would be the way of wisdom, for wisdom endeavours to see things in the largest possible context. Being able to laugh is a kind of wisdom, for as we have noted humour is able to perceive at least two separate things, what is as over against what ought to be – and the gap between them that usually shows up human folly. But the mysteries of life and death are not always funny. Death may also call for death, or for death a rebirth.

Chapter 11

Through Death to Life

Sacrifice and Atonement

Two mythic and religious scenarios come to mind when we think of the mysteries of death and life as passages on the road out of evil: sacrifice and initiation. Both involve death, the ending of the life or significance of an entity in one form, either symbolically or vicariously. Worshippers present offerings of fruit or grain or even money, or the death of an animal or even human victim in place of themselves; or undergo in their own persons symbolic death, though perhaps one entailing no little suffering as the price of real transformation.

First sacrifice. Sacrifice as atonement for evil is a central theme in religion, best known of course in the Christian narrative of Jesus on the cross. But making the proper sacrifice, not necessarily of oneself but perhaps of animal victims/substitutes, as in the biblical sacrifices performed by Noah and Job at the end of their ordeals, is very widespread as a way of 'making up' for evil in the sight of the divine; indeed, virtually every traditional religion demands some form of sacrifice, if not of life, then of effort, property or money. Often a myth presents the origin of the sacrifice, or interprets it, as in Hesiod, the Rig-Veda and the Chinese Book of Rites.

Purusha's Sacrifice

In the tenth book of the Rig-Veda, and in the ritual texts of the Brahmanas, Purusha (Prajapati in the Brahmanas) is identified as a kind of primal deity/primal man embracing all others, who made the world by offering himself as a sacrifice, so that his eyes become the sun and moon, his head the sky, his breath the wind, the many other parts of his body mountains, rivers, fields and so forth, of the world. We are also told that the four basic varnas or caste-groupings derived from him: the priestly brahmins from his head, the warrior kshatriya from his arms, the merchant and craftsman vaishyas from his belly, the peasant shudras from his legs. In the Brahmanas Prajapati is also said to have offered himself by means of the inner sacrifice of generating spiritual heat and power through *tapas*, extreme fasting, asceticism and concentration; from this cosmic force in turn derived *Brahman*, the universal energy, together with gods, humans and all other beings.

The texts also emphasize that sacrificial rituals offered by priests repeat Prajapati's primal sacrifice, and as it were reverse the original spreading-out of creation by restoring unity. Yogic *tapas* repeats the first deity's creation of the vast and many-formed cosmos; by seeing all that is as only Brahman taking many forms the mystic reintegrates the cosmos in the mind, making it again the One. The fire god Agni, central to Vedic sacrifice, is identified with Prajapati; licking tongues of flame consuming what is sacrificed makes it again one with primordial fire. So also did the brahmins' consumption of the sacred drink Soma, probably psychedelic, as its mind-expanding effects made the imbiber feel omniscient and omnipotent.[103]

The Sacrifices of Cain and Abel

Let us now turn to a different world of thought, that of the ancient Hebrews in the Near East. Here on the shores of the Mediterranean and in the deserts inland from that azure sea the practice of sacrifice may not have been highly different from in the foothills of the Himalayas or on the dusty plains of India. Types and methods of sacrifice: the offering of first-fruits of harvest, the use of all-destroying and purifying fire in the whole-burnt offering or holocaust, were all in all similar across the archaic world, though ritual words and details might vary. But the theological significance, one might say, of Vedic and Hebraic sacrifice differed as eminently as did their Gods and their created worlds.

For two views of divine creation emerge out of two scriptures, the Rig-Veda and the Bible. Compare the story of Purusha or Prajapati with that of Elohim, the world-maker in Genesis. The former tells us that God made the world out of himself, by dividing up his body in a primal sacrifice. The world then is like God in disguise, God playing hide-and-seek with himself, and if we want to find God we do not look into the heavens or beyond the stars, but to our own innermost nature, for we ourselves are fragments from that sacrificial act. This is the same view propounded in more philosophical language in the later Upanishads and Vedanta philosophy, insofar as it says that the atman, the essential human 'soul' or nature, is none other than Brahman, the universal divine essence.

But the Genesis account, at the beginning of the Bible, tells us that God created the world as it were from outside, like a carpenter making a box, seated above it as its Maker and calling very good his handiwork. This picture tells us that God is not to be identified with the creation, or with ourselves, our innermost nature or otherwise. In the traditional forms of the Western monotheistic religions, Judaism, Christianity and Islam, to say I *am* God is supreme blasphemy. We can have a deep relation of faith and love with God, but not one of identity.

Sacrifice in Vedic religion is, as we have seen, a gesture of restoring that original identity. In some forms of brahminic ritual it was making, as it were, technical adjustments which kept the One rolling smoothly along, or focusing the power of the One to some particular end, such as royal progeny or immortality. Clearly the offerings of Cain and Abel, though also meant to preserve concord between heaven and earth, were different in concept.

Taking the biblical account at face value, it seems that the first sacrifices were those offered by Cain and Abel, two brothers, sons of Adam and Eve. The rites must have occurred shortly after their parents' expulsion from the Garden of Eden, where presumably no sacrifice was necessary to maintain right relations between two unfallen humans and God, or to atone for sin not yet committed. Yet Cain and Abel must have sensed in some subjective way that, now that matters obviously were not square between heaven and earth, a token offering might be appropriate, to show that the pair of brothers had their Creator in mind as the source of all their bounty.

So we read that 'Abel was a keeper of sheep, and Cain a tiller of the ground. In the course of time Cain brought to the Lord an offering of the fruit of the ground, and Abel brought of the firstlings of his flock and of their fat portions.' (Gen 4: 2–4)

The story of how God accepted Abel's sacrifice but rejected Cain's, and how this led to the first murder, of Abel by Cain and the 'mark of Cain', is well known. But for the present purposes we will stop here, to consider what is meant by sacrifice to the Lord the best portion of that raised by the labour of one's hands, whether of field or flock.

First, this is not a repetition of a primal sacrifice, like that of Prajapati, or of the Aztecs who told of two gods who formed the universe by splitting a goddess in half; their violent acts of human sacrifice were a way of repaying the goddess and other deities for the violence of creation, making the severed again one. Nor was it like the Norse Odin, who self-sacrificed by hanging himself on the World Tree Yggdrasil for nine days to gain wisdom; for this reason war captives were sometimes hanged as offerings to Odin, known as the god of the hanged.

Theories concerning the meaning of sacrifice in the Hebrew scriptures are many and varied. Sacrifice is an expression of thanks to God; it is an offering to God in propitiation or atonement for one's sins; it is an exchange of life (the blood of the victim is the life) with the God who gave life; it is a communion with God if the offering is eaten, and a demonstration of one's dedication if it is not; it generates power concentrated in the victim itself that can then be applied elsewhere (e.g. in the sprinkling of blood of sacrifice on door lintels for protection); it is simply to be understood as an act of obedience to divine command.

The relation of sacrifice to fertility is evident in many archaic agricultural societies. The males of the Jivaroan tribes of the Upper Amazon, headhunters and headshrinkers, would perform a dance in the fields with the head and two female relatives, usually sister and wife; he would hold the shrunken head by its hair in his outstretched hand, while the two women held on to him or the other, from behind. It was as though power was flowing from the head through the three dancers into the crops.[104] Others have simply placed human or animal sacrificial victims on stakes around the fields, or buried parts of the bodies in them.

Returning to the offerings of Cain and Abel, they seem best understood as acts of thanksgiving, recognizing that giving thanks through concrete means establishes an invaluable link with God. But it is also clear that God only accepts sacrifices made with clean hands and a pure heart. The rejection of Cain's offering undoubtedly reflects the age-old rivalry between pastoral nomads and settled agriculturalists. The ancient Hebrews, wandering with their flocks from place to place, would have aligned themselves with Abel and his nomadic kind. But the text itself – God telling Cain, 'If you do well, will you not be accepted?' – suggests that Cain also harboured some fault within himself, a notion certainly reinforced by his subsequent turning to anger and the murder of Abel rather than reformation. Biblical sacrifice then is transaction between two independent parties, though one looms far greater than the other. Yet the two each have standing that must be articulated and proven. The offering is a means of giving thanks, of establishing a relationship to God, and then puts to test one's own worthiness.

Nancy Jay, in *Throughout Your Generations Forever: Sacrifice, Religion, and Paternity*, a study of sacrifice, primarily but not entirely biblical, has emphasized still another note: the role of sacrifice in confirming kinship or covenanted relationships, particularly among males.[105] She notes first that blood sacrifice is generally a male activity, and although women may sometimes assist, as in certain Vedic rituals, childbearing women never do; while giving life one does not also take life. Very common, on the other hand, are sacrifices involving father and son, or sacrificial oblations to male ancestors, or male groups establishing kinship or treaty obligations. The blood of sacrifice stands over against the blood of menstruation and childbirth in women, often seen as polluting. This blood mandates ritually what women have by nature in giving birth: a solemn relationship sealed by blood, giving power and establishing lines of descent.

This role of sacrifice can be seen in the Hebrew scriptures. It could be argued that Cain's offering was rejected because it did not involve blood, and therefore the lineage leading to Noah and Abraham stemmed not from him, though he had descendants, but through Seth, a third son Adam and Eve had to replace the murdered Abel. Moreover, before God promised Abraham descendants and the promised land, he commanded him to offer sacrifice of a heifer, a she-goat, a ram, a turtledove and a young pigeon, and to cut the three animals (not the birds) in half; a rite sometimes called the cutting of the covenant. Then, in a very mysterious nighttime scene, after making his promise, God caused fire to pass between the separated pieces. (Gen. 15: 7–21) Much more, including Abraham's almost-sacrifice of his son Isaac, could be adduced to illustrate the relationship between sacrifice and male lineage in the Bible and elsewhere; in effect these accounts serve as mythical prototypes for the sacrificial cultus of Israel.

At the same time, it must be acknowledged that sacrifice is one of those religious practices in which the mode of performance is more consistent than the theoretical or mythical explanation. As we have seen, sacrifice has been given a number of rationales. What can be affirmed is that, in every case, it seems to express the idea of death for life. By one killing, the sins of another are expiated to allow that person or persons to live more freely; power is released to afford protection or fertility; a life-enhancing relationship with God is made; a male lineage is sanctified.

Initiation

Initiation scenarios no less establish a relationship and put the candidate to the test. But in this case the sacrificial victim was the candidate himself, though – if all went well – virtually rather than actually. Human initiation usually models self-sacrificial death and rebirth. It is also a way of reversing and overcoming evil, even though, as we have seen in a previous chapter, the ordeal can also be a source of evil when it implies that the initiate has been brought into a state 'beyond good and evil'.

Religious initiation may be general in a society, into a sacred lodge or order, to shamanistic or religious office, as disciple of a spiritual leader, or in some cases even as individual spiritual experience interpreted as equivalent to an initiation. Generally a myth goes with an initiation, sometimes solemnly imparted during the ceremony, which explains its origin and purpose. Initiation is a counter to evil in that it explains it in some fashion, and gives the initiate a strong sense of having received power to combat it. Examples are shamanistic initiations, the initiation into the mysteries of Isis in Apuleius, the training of the Zen monk.

Shamanism

The Siberian shaman was usually called through the violent means of a seizure or fit, often involving running about, frothing, crying out, and then unnatural lassitude and deep sleep. The great pioneer of Siberian ethnography Marie Antoinette Czaplicka, stated that prospective shamans often have violent seizures in which they lie motionless two or three days without food.[106] In this period in which the apprentice is outside ordinary time, a god may speak to him about his vocation. On the other hand, in the Americas the candidate is particularly likely to be called by an animal spirit: by an otter among the Tlingit; an eagle, coyote or horned owl among the California Maricopa.[107]

Then comes a long process of initiation into shamanhood. While the apprentice may work under a senior shaman, much of his time will probably be alone, or alone with his own ancillary spirit. The Eskimo or Inuit shaman's experience of receiving his angakok or spirit-guide has been vividly described:

> The angakok consists of a mysterious light which the shaman suddenly feels in his body, inside his head, within the brain, an inexplicable searchlight, a luminous fire, which enables him to see in the dark, both literally and metaphorically speaking, for he can now, even with closed eyes, see through darkness and perceive things and coming events, which are hidden from others: thus they look into the future and into the secrets of others.
>
> The candidate obtains this mystical light after long hours of waiting, sitting on a bench in his hut and invoking the spirits. When he experiences it for the first time 'it is as if the house in which he is suddenly rises; he sees far ahead of him, through mountains, exactly as if the earth were one great plain, and his eyes could reach to the end of the earth. Nothing is hidden from him any longer; not only can he see things far, far away, but he can also discover souls, stolen souls, which are either kept concealed in far, strange lands, or have been taken up or down to the Land of the Dead.'[108]

The Eskimo shaman Igjugarjuk said to the Danish explorer Knud Rasmussen:

> All true wisdom is only found far from men, out in the great solitude, and it can be acquired only through suffering. Privations and suffering are the only things that can open a man's mind to that which is hidden from others.[109]

In some cases, as among the Yakut, the initiation reportedly involved cutting up the body of the future shaman and counting his bones; if there were not enough, he could not become a shaman, or perhaps one of his relatives would have to die to make up the lack.

Yet all of this happened during sickness, or in the heavens, or while the candidate was alone with the gods and spirits in the great wilderness, and followed the mythical model of the great shamans at the beginning. Among the Buryat of Siberia it was said that the novice was instructed by dead shamanistic ancestors, who take him to heaven, where he is boiled so as to become 'fully cooked', that is, mature, as a shaman. In antiquity, they say, all shamans were so prepared. While this is going on, the shaman lies for seven days as though dead, and his family sings, 'Our shaman will come back to life, he will set us free.'[110]

Thus the initiation of the shaman, extreme as it may seem, is a path to reversing the evil of the world, and lead us on the way into freedom.

The Mysteries of Isis

In the days when Rome ruled the world, many religions streamed in from its far corners to plant temples in its imperial cities. Among them was the cultus of Isis, the great goddess of Egypt. In Egyptian myth, Isis, mother of magic, was consort of Osiris, deity of fertility and immortality. When he was killed and dismembered by Set, the sinister god representing the hot wind of the desert, Isis wandered the world assembling his remains, finally bringing them back to life by her magic long enough to impregnate her with Horus, their divine son.

In the Hellenistic world, Isis became identified with the Greek Demeter, the great mother who sought her daughter Persephone as far as the Underworld, and indeed with Ishtar, Artemis and the Great Mother of a thousand names around the earth. So the Latin writer Apuleius, as Lucius, described her, going on to tell of his vision of the goddess: 'A woman began to rise from the middle of the sea with so lovely a face that the gods themselves would have fallen down in adoration of it . . . Just above her brow shone a round disc, like a mirror, or like the bright face of the moon, which told me who she was.'[111] The radiant deity then tells him she will change him back from the body of an ass into which he has been transformed; in thanksgiving for this blessing he would be initiated into her mysteries.

The priest who was to perform the initiation made plain that this ordeal was in the hands of Isis, and was a test of the candidate; one should not seek supreme initiation without direct orders from the Goddess. 'The gates of the Underworld and the guardianship of life are in her hands, and the rites of initiation approximate to a voluntary death from which there is only a precarious hope of resurrection.'[112] Yet the day came when Lucius was called to initiation. Though he says he is not allowed to give full details, he tells enough to whet the reader's curiosity, and to indicate that the nocturnal rite re-enacted Demeter's journey to the Underworld to retrieve Persephone (Proserpine in Latin), and undoubtedly likewise to represent Isis's search for the scattered body of Osiris:

I approached the very gates of death and set one foot on Proserpine's threshold, yet was permitted to return, rapt through all the elements. At midnight I saw the sun shining as if it were noon; I entered the presence of the gods of the underworld and the gods of the upperworld, stood near and worshiped them.[113]

This initiation was manifestly a positive transformation for Lucius, letting him leave behind the evil symbolized by the donkey's body in which he was trapped. Afterwards, he voluntarily stayed some days, he says, in the goddess's temple, full of joy and contemplating her statue.

Zen Initiation

Finally, consider how the initiation of the Zen monk in Japan is both a transition to and a foretaste of the novice's new way of life. First, the young man must leave home for the monastery, on what is known as *anga* or 'going on foot', even though today the journey may in fact be by modern modes of transportation. But undoubtedly in the old days, when the home-leaving might mean walking for a number of days, wearing only a rough robe and straw sandals, with no more supplies than one could carry in a small pack on one's back, getting there was itself a significant part of the experience of changing from one life to another. It was the commencement of the traditional real purpose of Zen, 'seeing into one's true nature', above all by stripping away all that is superimposed over that true nature: comforts, attachments to place, to family, even to one's original name. Zen makes all these anew in its austere way.

When he finally knocks on the monastery door, he is politely but firmly refused admission. He will be told this monastery is too full, too poor or too harsh to take him. He is left outside the entrance, where he sits in a semblance of the Zen meditation posture, as though unwilling to accept the rebuff, but is merely pushed away rudely by anyone coming or going who finds him in the way.

Eventually, come evening, he will be invited in 'for one night only' to sleep on the hard floor of an ante-room. But the next day he will find this was in fact the beginning of probation of some five days he will spend in the ante-room, practising the correct method of Zen meditation and other monastic disciplines. Afterwards, he will be admitted to the zendo or main meditation hall to join his future fellow monks.

His formal entry to the zendo may be celebrated by the traditional Japanese tea ceremony, long associated with Zen.

In time he may, in an interview with the roshi or Zen master, be given a koan, one of those enigmatic Zen sayings on which the monk focusing thought while doing zazen, or Zen sitting: 'What is the sound of one hand?' 'What was your face before you were born?'[114]

Perhaps at some point he will experience satori or kensho, a flash of enlightenment, of seeing his true nature as the Buddha-nature, as the Buddha knew him at the moment of his enlightenment, and at the same time see all nature as it truly is, empty, infinitely interconnected and marvellous.

This pattern was established some twenty-five centuries ago, according to Buddhist tradition, by the Buddha himself, when he left his palatial home on his great spiritual quest, leaving behind that his past. Finally, after many trials, he entered into fully awakened consciousness. He was a hero on the spiritual plane, and it is to the hero emergent out of evil to whom we must turn next.

Chapter 12

The Hero Victorious

Who Fights and Why?

The hero needs to fight an adversary. As we have noted, this requisite could be seen as an interpretation of evil – the hero's necessary dragon. Now we move into accounts of individual heroes who battled in some way to counter the tide of evil, in the process showing a way out.

First come the champion/hero like Hercules, the Japanese Yamatotakeru, or the Tibetan epic figure Gesar who defeat particular evils in the course of episodic narratives. Modern examples range from comic book or cinematic 'superheroes' to historical personages who have become legends (in some circles), like Kit Carson or Napoleon.

While the champion does little against evil as a general condition, and sometimes seems quite flawed, this kind of fighter does present the possibility of individual struggle, and of making a difference in a finite sphere. The champion may be female, like the Polynesian Hina. Modern examples include such comic-book and cinematic characters as the Lone Ranger, Superman and Batman, who share numerous characteristics with the heroes of classic myth, beginning with unusual or extraterrestrial birth.

The 'quester' as heroic figure is not limited to a picaresque kind of campaign against evil, but like Jason seeking for Golden Fleece, or knights of Camelot for the Holy Grail, or Dorothy trying to find the way out of Oz back to Kansas, may be identified with a sustained effort towards a supreme goal. Again, the labour may not result, or be intended to result, in a final defeat of evil. Theirs is another story from that of the hero as champion. In both instances, the paradigmatic myth of the hero, with its steps such as unusual birth, call, initiation, ordeal and triumph, is a definite antithesis to the myth of evil coming into the world. Indeed, a case could be made that one significant way of understanding evil is that it makes possible the hero's adventure, as a model of human life. The saviour is a figure in the mould of the hero, champion or quester, who exhibits a similar life-pattern. But he defeats evil worldwide in principle, though at present only inwardly through faith, devotion or meditation, rather than in outward battle. Broadly speaking, founding personalities of the great religions, Moses, Jesus, Zarathustra, the Buddha, Confucius and Muhammad, as well as such others as Orpheus or Krishna, are in this pattern if not always saviours in a theological sense.

The Champion

The champion is the hero who, like Beowulf, Arjuna, David, Hercules or Achilles, is a fighter of heroic proportions. He is not identified with a single great quest, like Jason for the Golden Fleece or Sir Galahad for the Holy Grail. The champion's story is more on the model of a picaresque: a series of only loosely related events in which he displays his cunning and daring, but which do not add up to a single triumph and reward. He seems to be guided by a kind of irresistible fate, together with a love of action for its own sake, more than by any particular goal. This hero does not look far ahead, but puts all his strength and cunning into prevailing where he is engaged at the moment. Sometimes he may look more like a brawler who loves a good fight, and his own reputation as the toughest fellow around, more than any loftier values, but his escapades make for great stories, as well as usually reflecting attributes his own people see as among their salient qualities.

Hercules (or Herakles in Greek) is one of the best-known examples. Like many of the greatest heroes, he was born half-divine and half-human, his mother having been 'loved' by Zeus; however this affair, like the many other amours of the king of the gods, enraged the Olympian's wife Hera, who from Hercules' infancy on up tried to thwart or kill the hero. (Nonetheless Herakles enigmatically means 'Glory of Hera'.) Hercules destroyed two serpents sent by the Olympian queen to his cradle, and later as a young man fought with wild beast, centaurs and amazons, and assisted Jason in the quest of the Golden Fleece. His triumphs owed as much to the clever stratagems as to brute strength.

But then Hercules killed his wife and children in a mad rage brought on by Hera; in penance he was sent by the oracle of Delphi to a certain Eurystheus, who assigned him the famous twelve labours. These gradually extending out from Greece to the farthest fringes of the Hellenic world, ranged from fighting the Nemean lion and the nine-headed Hydra, to seeking the golden apples of the Hesperides in the far west, to fetching up the three-headed dog Cerberus who guarded the underworld.

Finally, Hercules was killed in a strange way. He had shot a centaur, Nessus, who had tried to rape his second wife, Deianeira. But the dying half-man, half-horse told the hero's wife that if he soaked Hercules' shirt in his blood and semen, it would keep him faithful. Instead, when Hercules put it on, it caused him to die in agony – and to be killed by one's wife, even if unintentionally, would have been considered very shameful in ancient Greece. Nevertheless, when the spirit of Hercules was taken to Olympus, he became a god, a very rare honour for a figure even half mortal. But though flawed, this son of Zeus seemed even to the gods themselves to possess a certain magnificence that outshone his faults.

So it is that the hero as champion on his own level finds victory over his adversaries the means to self-realization as divine. While no doubt the serpents of his infancy, the Nemean lion, and the Hydra, were acting only out of innocent instinct, they are portrayed mythically as evil insofar as they defy human hegemony, and it is the hero's task as protector of humanity as well as exemplar of his own virtue to defeat or destroy them. So it is that Hercules fights his way to Mt Olympus, home of the gods.

Somewhat similar is Yamato-takeru, 'Strong Man of Yamato', a figure in Japanese mythology. [Yamato, the area around Nara and Kyoto, was the ancient centre of Japanese civilization.] Originally named Prince Ousu, he was son of the Emperor Keiko, who reigned in the 4th century CE according to the traditional chronology. Yamato-takeru was sent by that sovereign to combat rebels in various distant parts of the Island Empire as he sought to unify his realm. In this task the prince was assisted by two women, his aunt Princess Yamato, high priestess of the Grand Shrine of Ise, dedicated to the goddess Amaterasu, ancestress of the imperial line; and his lovely wife Ototachibana, who faithfully accompanied him on his missions, but whom he did not treat with appropriate affection until too late.

The mythology of the *Kojiki* (712 CE, and the oldest extant Japanese book) presents him as a violent figure who slew his elder brother, and whose royal father then sent him on a mission to combat rebels in the southern island of Kyushu. The prince's forces were greatly outnumbered, and the ruler clearly expected his unruly son would be killed in return for the fratricide. But on the way he visited his aunt, Princess Yamato, high priestess at Ise. She made him a gift of a fine silken garment – woman's clothes. Then, assisted by his wife the Princess Ototachibana, Prince Ousu cleverly disguised himself in them as a beautiful maiden who made herself welcome at a party of the adversaries, where he won the drunken affections of the enemy chieftain. As he attempted to press 'her' closer to himself, the Yamato hero dispatched the outlaw with a concealed dagger. Learning too late who his murderer was, in his dying breath the foeman named him Yamato-takeru, 'Yamato strongman'.

The imperial scion used another deceitful stratagem dealing with the captain of dissidents in Izumo. Challenging that adversary to single combat, Yamato-takeru gave him a wooden imitation sword which could not even be removed from its scabbard, while keeping one of fine steel for himself; the unfortunate victim of this 'joke' was quickly slain.

The emperor nonetheless remained displeased with his son, sending the prince now East to deal with further rebels. But again visiting his aunt at the Ise shrine on the way, he was now given the holy sword he would soon name Kusanagi ('grass-cutter'); this was the same blade which Susanoo, brother of Amaterasu, had found in a dragon that the storm-god had slain. The priestess also presented Yamato-takeru with a bag of flints, the purpose of which her nephew did not know at the moment.

Once again Yamato-takeru, despite his great strength, disingenuously used fained friendship as a ploy, as on this occasion did his adversaries also. The eastern rebels at first professed hospitality, as did the distinguished visitor. They feasted one another in turn.

Then one day the supposed comrades invited their imperial guest on a hunt. But when he was in the field alone, suddenly he found himself surrounded by a raging fire; manifestly he had been ambushed and the enemy expected the emperor's son to be incinerated. However, taking out the flint given him by the priestess, Yamato-takeru created a backfire to protect himself, while using the sacred blade to slice down the taller grass, and when the flames had died down, he walked out unscathed. Then using the sword to slice down men as well as foliage, Yamato-takeru won the day.

Later, on yet another mission, Yamato-takeru and his men had to cross a strait in a small boat. The hero was as usual accompanied by his wife Ototachibana, and despite the fact that he had lately been infatuated by another, younger princess, she remained utterly loyal to him. Indeed, as a storm arose – allegedly because of the boastful words of Yamato-takeru that this stretch of sea was nothing and could be crossed easily, which the local sea-god took as an insult – it appeared the boat would be sunk. But Ototachibana then offered herself as a sacrifice to the sea-god.

Pacified, the deity relented. But Yamato-takeru, though he then made it safely to shore, was totally devastated by his wife's death, and penitent over his previous treatment of her. In the mountains he accidentally killed a white deer, which reminded him of her – white being associated with death in East Asia. Moreover, he kept getting lost in the white deathlike mist which enveloped those highlands, once having to be led out of the befogged mazelike hills by a white dog.

Though he then married the princess with whom he had been infatuated, Yamato-takeru remained in mourning, and his own death came soon after. Sent to rescue the people of Omi from a huge serpent, he strangled it easily enough with his bare hand. But then a great mountain god in the form of a white boar, whose minion the serpent was, in vengeance sent sickness to the powerful but all-too-human hero. Though in his illness he tried to return to his father, he died near Ise before he reached home, saying with final philosophical insight that time passes like a coach past a crack in a wall. The emperor Keiko, reconciled and remorseful, had a great burial mound erected for his heroic son at that spot. But it is said that his soul then took the form of a great white bird which flew on back to Yamato, the land of his birth.[115]

Like Hercules, Yamato-takeru had many faults; he was clever to the point of unscrupulousness, boastful, callous towards women until too late, and prone to a hot temper and excessive violence. Like Odysseus, he was famous for the sort of lying deception which moralists would castigate, yet which in both cases make for entertaining stories beloved by countless hearers and readers. Moreover, the Japanese prince was manifestly the sort of leader who evokes great loyalty. In the end, his cunning strength and magnificent exploits made him seem more than human. If Hercules became a god of Olympus, Yamato-takeru is ranked as one of the Shinto kami or deities.

The Questing Hero and the Way Back

The champion's career is like a one-thing-after-another story, loosely bound together by the personality and qualities of the hero. But in that of the quester all the parts are linked by an ultimate purpose. She or he seeks a final goal: Jason and the Golden Fleece, Odysseus returning to Ithaca, Frodo destroying the Ring of Power, Dorothy getting back home to Kansas. Furthermore, the journey may include scenes and places of fabulous, transcendent beauty or 'otherness', like Oz, that suggest movement beyond the circles of this world: palaces of gold or diamond, soaring mountains, magical – perhaps talking – beasts. The quest moves towards its singular goal, but on the way transforms the participants, perchance making them less of this world with all its evil.

Digressions and distractions may, to be sure, lie along the way as well as exaltation. They both have their place, so long as the traveller does not get wholly lost. The modern Greek poet C. P. Cavafy wrote with Odysseus in mind in 'Ithaka':

> When you set out for Ithaka
> pray that your road's a long one,
> full of adventure, full of discovery.
> Laistrygonians, Cyclops,
> angry Poseidon – don't be scared of them:
> you won't find things like that on your way
> as long as your thoughts are exalted,
> as long as a rare excitement
> stirs your spirit and your body.[116]

An excellent example of all this is the Russian tale of Prince Ivan, a story also often called 'Three Kingdoms'. A king (or tsar) married a beautiful queen, by whom he had three sons: Piotr, Vasily and Ivan. All went well until one day the queen, walking in a palace garden, was swept away by a great whirlwind.

Later, the day came when the three boys had reached manhood. The king, still sorrowing over his loss, sent his sons out to search for their mother. But no sooner had they left the palace grounds than Ivan, the youngest, asked the others if he could make his quest alone. The others tried to dissuade him, but without success, and finally the two older youths went their way without him.

Ivan reached a deep forest. There, in a clearing, he met an old man who listened to his story. Feeling sympathy for the boy bereft of his mother, the old man – clearly a wizard of some kind – gave him a ball, saying that if he kept rolling it before him, it would lead him to her.

Ivan did that, and the ball led him to great mountain of iron and a mighty cave within it. Ivan entered the cave and climbed upward within the mountain for a month before he came out onto a high ledge, where he saw a castle of copper in the far distance. The young explorer went towards it, only to find its gate guarded by hissing serpents. But pacifying them with water from a nearby well, he went in, where he met the queen of the copper castle. She was not able to tell him about his mother, but she said she was a victim of the whirlwind as well, gave him a copper ball as his guide, and asked him to free her as well on his return.

The adventure was repeated twice more, as Ivan was led to silver and gold castles, each guarded by vicious serpents who could be distracted by water. Each housed a sad abducted queen, each more beautiful than the one before, who each gave the hero a guiding ball and begged to be freed on his return.

Finally, the golden ball led him to a diamond castle, patrolled by serpents with six heads. There he found, enthroned but imprisoned, his mother. She embraced him with joy, but warned her son he was in great danger. He would, she said, have to defeat the whirlwind in battle. She showed him two vats of water in the cellar, one the Water of Strength, the other plain. Ivan drank of the former, then as his mother cleverly suggested, switched the two.

Soon the whirlwind returned, and on entering the castle became a handsome man who tried to kiss his captive bride. But Ivan sprang forward to challenge the whirlwind-villain. They fought across the world until finally, growing tired, the abdicator returned to the castle to replenish himself from the Water of Strength. But because of the exchange he became only weaker, and Ivan, sipping from the other vat, felt a burst of fresh energy. He was then able to kill the opponent, burning his body and scattering his ashes to the winds.

The triumphant youngest son made his way back home, rescuing the other queens on the way. Omitting further adventures found in some versions, involving treachery against Ivan on the part of his older brothers, we will now move to the happy ending: the king and queen were reunited; Ivan married the golden queen; Piotr and Vasily respectively married the silver and copper queens.

What can be said about this narrative? Certainly, it could be analysed from a Freudian psychoanalytic perspective: consider the basic quest for the mother, guarded by phallic serpents, victory coming only after battle with a figure who seems at once a rival male and primordial chaos. Or take the Jungian slant: Ivan, as the youngest son, could well stand for the marvellous child representing individuation as well as the hero in the hero's quest. In the process he is aided by, and so reconciled with, the major positive archetypes: the wizard as Wise Old Man, his mother as Great Mother, the three queens, including his prospective wife, as Maiden; while the whirlwind can only be the Shadow, whose power one can learn to control and even use against him.

However, our major interest now is in the hero as prototype of one moving beyond the realm of evil altogether. It may seem that too many magical events occur in this story to make it humanly convincing; that Ivan is little more than a passive figure to whom things happen enabling him to move on to a foreordained conclusion. However, Ivan's perseverance, and willingness to take advantage of what help comes his way, is surely also a part of the story. The magic does show a quality also important to religion and myth alike. It tells us that we live in a marvellous, many-layered world, in which some events happen by human choice, but others are beyond human control or even full human understanding; the true hero must be prepared for both. Furthermore, in the world of religion and myth, other agencies than the human are at play; some seek to help, and some to hinder, the hero; with this too she or he must come to terms. All this Ivan seems to understand, or at least under pressure of adventure to learn.

The Sage and Saviour as Hero

Finally, let us recall again that not all heroes combat evil with sword of steel in hand. There are also those who fight wielding the sword of the spirit, meeting adversaries with wisdom or with the power of love. Among these are saints, sages and saviours of all religions. We have looked at the Buddha as mythic hero, making comparisons with Jesus and others among the great religious founders. (Again, the term myth is not used to imply judgement on the historicity of these lives, but to indicate congruity with the mythic model of the hero.) Now let us take the example of Mahavira ('Great Hero', his title in Jainism), founder of the Jain religion, probably an older contemporary of the Buddha.[117] Indeed, the parallels between the lives of the two great ascetics and wise teachers are such that many early Western scholars mistakenly took them to be variant versions of the same individual's life.

Mahavira (c. 599–527 BCE; some scholars put his dates about a half century later) was born as Vardhamana, the younger son of a local king, like the family of the Buddha, members of the kshatriya caste. That caste of rulers and warriors was in considerable tension at the time with the priestly brahmins, resenting their claims to exclusive spiritual power and their demands for cattle and other materials with which to perform their Vedic sacrifices. The teaching of both Mahavira and Buddha (as well as the Bhagavad Gita) emphasizes that the Vedic scriptures and rituals to which the brahmins held custodianship were not necessary to liberation, but that freedom could be found equally well inwardly by a non-brahmin through asceticism and meditation, or by following one's duty (*dharma*) without attachment to the fruits of action.

Mahavira is believed by Jains to be the twenty-fourth in a series of *tirthankaras* ('ford-makers', in the sense of a ford for crossing a river), teachers who have appeared at great intervals in the world. His birth is said to have followed a series of auspicious dreams on the part of his mother, and that even in the womb he practised *ahimsa* (harmlessness, a great Jaina virtue), striving to cause his mother no pain.

His parents are reported to have been very devout, themselves practising asceticism. Nonetheless, the boy, like the Buddha, was raised in luxury, married and had a child, in his case a daughter. But at age thirty, after his parents had died, he renounced the world, distributing his property, pulling out his hair. He lived the hard life of a wandering celibate monk, begging his food, living under trees or wherever he could, after a time giving up clothes to go naked or 'sky-clad' like the Digambara order of Jain monks, so as to own no possessions whatsoever. (The other order, the Svetambara, retains light robes; there are some differences in the biography of the religion's founder as told by the two communities.) Above all, Mahavira exercised *ahimsa*, harmlessness, towards all creatures, even allowing insects to crawl on his body, and enduring taunts and abuse for his uncouthness. Nonetheless he acquired disciples and began teaching.

Then, some twelve years after his departure from home, by a tree on the banks of a river, the great renunciant attained *kevala-jnana*, or full knowledge, in which his consciousness is said to have become infinite, so that he knew the condition of all beings: past, present and future. The basic Jain teaching, of which he undoubtedly uttered the essence, is that sentient, feeling life dwells in all that exists: gods, humans, animals, plants, even stones, dust and air. These *jivas*, souls or particles of life, are entrapped in the material shells of these substances as a result of *karma*.

The Jain view of *karma* is somewhat different from the Hindu or Buddhist; for Jains it is more like a material coating that covers souls as a consequence of action based on desire and thereby condemns them to the suffering incumbent upon material existence. Since it is action that created the covering, its opposite, non-action, meditation and above all the stoic enduring of suffering and pain, including that incumbent in *ahimsa*, wears it off; in time the ascetic then reduces the karmic coat to nothing, so that he or she breaks through to *kevala*, liberation, and after dropping the body ascends to an eternal nirvana above. But inflicting suffering on another soul, whether through cruelty or indifference or even apparent necessity, adds to one's burden of *karma*. For this reason, Jains go to great lengths to counter the callousness of the world towards life. Virtually all Jains are strict vegetarians and go so far as to put screens around lamps to keep insects from flying into them. Many Jain temples maintain homes for unwanted animals and hospitals for injured birds.

After his enlightenment, Mahavira preached to great crowds, and founded the Jain faith with its orders of monks dedicated to strict practices leading to liberation, and its laypeople devoted at least to a life in which new karmic burdens would not be added. One early disciple, Gosala, is said to have left him to lead the Ajivaka (deterministic materialism) sect. Finally, at age seventy-two, Mahavira himself entered nirvana.

Like the lives of Moses, Krishna, the Buddha and Jesus, Mahavira's story exhibits exceptional birth, leaving home in order to fulfil a spiritual vocation, a period of preparatory suffering and no doubt temptation, final initiation (Jesus' baptism, the Buddha's enlightenment, the last *tirthankara*'s attaining infinite wisdom), a period of teaching, betrayal or at least abandonment by a follower, and after death entry into an ultimate state. The hero, whether of battle inner or outer, has a fascinating dual role in regard to the problem of evil: on the one hand evil can be seen as necessary to his victory; on the other, that victory shows, figuratively or literally, the way out.

Chapter 13

The Meaning of War

Why Do We Do What We Say We Hate?

A remarkable autobiographical novel, *Storm of Steel*, is based on the author's life as a German soldier in World War I. Ernst Jünger's vivid narrative depicts not only the endless anxious tedium, the fear, the sickening horror of what is seen and done on the battlefield, but also moments of another kind. In the midst of one engagement:

> I was to observe that there is a quality of dread that feels as unfamiliar as a foreign country. In moments when I felt it, I experienced no fear as such but a kind of exalted, almost demoniacal lightness; often attended by fits of laughter I was unable to repress.[118]

Commencing the great offensive of March 1918:

> The immense desire to destroy that overhung the battlefield precipitated a red mist in our brains. We called out sobbing and stammering fragments of sentences to one another, and an impartial observer might have concluded that we were all ecstatically happy.[119]

But a little later, after he had killed an 'enemy':

> Outside [a dugout] lay my British soldier, little more than a boy, who had been hit in the temple. He lay there, looking quite relaxed. I forced myself to look closely at him. It wasn't a case of 'you or me' any more. I often thought back on him and more with the passing of the years. The state, which relieves us of our responsibility,

cannot take away our remorse; and we must exercise it. Sorrow, regret pursued me deep in into my dreams.[120]

And finally, when he was shot, and believed, wrongly as it turned out, that he had himself been killed:

> Strangely, that moment is one of very few in my life of which I am able to say they were utterly happy. I understood, as in a flash of lightning, the true inner purpose and form of my life. I felt surprise and disbelief that it was to end there and then, but this surprise had something untroubled and almost merry about it. Then I heard the firing grow less, as if I were a stone sinking under the surface of some turbulent water. Where I was going, there was neither war nor enmity.[121]

War calls up some of the most extreme feelings and experiences imaginable, both of rapture and horror. Some, because other human happenings, such as honeymoons and giving birth, are unlikely to occur in connection with the deadly adventures of battle. War covers another part of the spectrum, one centring on males, their relationships and preoccupations. These may mimic, but will not entirely equate with, the gentler arts that also involve women.

Contrasting passages in *Storm of Steel*, as well as in other equally famous novels of war, such as Stephan Crane's *The Red Badge of Courage*, Erich Maria Remarque's *All Quiet on the Western Front*, or Norman Mailer's *The Naked and the Dead*, illumine sundry such features of the trooper's life: not only the fear and manic exaltation of the front, but also the intense bonding of warrior comrades, the almost frantically-seized lulls or leaves when relaxation is possible, even occasional flirting with young women behind the lines. But as anyone who has been there knows, both then and in the dreams of years later, war takes us to the heart. Of evil? Of a way through and beyond evil?

No study of the mythology of evil, its causes and cure in the realm of story, could be complete without a consideration of war. And war is, again, a matter of extreme paradox. Without minimizing other forms of human evil, it can surely be said that rarely if ever do they create war's sheer quantity of suffering and death. For war is intended to produce, deliberately, the killing and maiming of humans by other humans on a victorious scale, together with vast destruction of human artefacts, devastation now on the magnitude of entire cities. Not only that, but Mars leaves in his grisly wake sorrow, famine, plague and the ruination beyond measure of those who have survived.

Yet, at the same time, war is the one large-scale source of evil officially recognized by societies and its institutions, both political and religious. Its formal commencement, by declaration of war or the equivalent, officially and (in the eyes of society) morally gives participants permission to do that killing, maiming, and destroying, not to mention robbery and the practice of deceit (in espionage, propaganda, strategy, etc.), then allowed but not otherwise, as Jünger recognized when he said the state relieved him of that responsibility, though not the remorse. Yet even remorse may be mitigated insofar as participation in war is widely regarded as a source of pride, honour and glory. What is homicide, otherwise, makes heroes in war.

How then can we understand the human propensity for warfare, despite the general condemnation of its terrible nature? Why do we do what we know is both near absolute evil and near absolute glory? It is not our intention here to investigate the whole issue of the causes of war, only those aspects of it suggested by mythical models. But these are significant enough to show why war has a persistent fascination for humans, and why the credo of a war to end war is disconfirmed in the end, as the drama of war calls for encores over and over. We shall begin with, in myth, the first war.

War in Heaven

In the beginning, Michael and his angels warred against the minions of Satan, ultimately casting those rebels out of the courts of God. The Christian drama of this conflict is celebrated most famously in John Milton's *Paradise Lost*. The splendour of this primal battle of righteous archangelic sword raised against evil has inspired not a few Christian fighting-men down through the ages. In the Middle Ages, Christian knighthood saw itself as dedicated above all to St Michael, and in northern Europe shrines of that commander of the hosts of heaven were frequently at sites once sacred to Wotan.

The pagan deity, king of the warrior Aesir, had fought his own battle of the beginning. Even now Wotan, 'the father of slaughter, God of desolation and fire, the active and roaring deity, he who giveth victory, and reviveth courage in the conflict, and nameth those who are slain',[122] could often be heard of a strange and mysterious night thundering through the skies with his companions on the 'wild hunt'. Although details are unclear, at the beginning the two sets of Nordic gods, the Aesir of Wotan and his second-in-command Thor, given to war, magic and the sky, fought against the Vanir, lords over land, sea and fertility, in a long and brutal struggle. After it, although the Aesir maintained their sovereignty, a few Vanir, including Njord, god of the sea, and Freyr and Freya, deities of peace and abundance, were allowed to dwell at Asgard, home of the Aesir.

It is significant that those dubbed Christian knights, consecrated to take part in those wars the church considered just, were in a lineage of war dating from days of myth, whether symbolized by the hammer of Thor or the sword of St Michael; we will look at knightly initiation in a moment.

Here is another interesting model related to the primal war. The war in heaven at the beginning of the world is repeated at the end. Many readers will be familiar with the battle of Armageddon, based on a rather obscure New Testament passage (Rev. 16: 16), but which has entered Christian folklore as a symbol of armies gathered for a final battle before the End, as if it were a 'book-end' reflection of the primal war of St Michael against Satan.

In Zoroastrianism, the saviour-figure Saoshyant will appear at the end of the last age to defeat evil and prepare for the resurrection of the dead; in Hinduism, at the end of the Kaliyuga, the last and worst period in the repeating cycle of world ages, the avatar Kalki will appear as a warrior on a white horse to battle for the saving of those who can still be saved. (The white horse is a recurring motif in this drama: he is the mount of Christ in Rev. 19: 11–19, of Saoshyant, Kalki and in Tibetan myth of the king of Shambhala, Rudrachakrin, who will ride forth on such a steed to defeat evil at the end of the age.)

The Battle for Kingship

Wheeling back to the beginning again, let us now examine the relation of primal hostilities to the establishment of human society. In the Babylonian mythology described in Chapter 4, order emerged after the heroic deity Marduk fought Tiamat, the goddess/sea-monster who represented primordial chaos. He and she were each supported by a squadron of gods or demons. What is particularly significant about this struggle is that, before going into engagement, Marduk demanded the other gods on his side agree to cede him absolute power as king if he were successful; this they did, knowing full well that none of *them* was able to confront the rampaging goddess disquieting the universe.

After his victory, as we have seen, Marduk went on to divide Tiamat in two, making heaven of her upper half and earth of the lower. He formed the land of Mesopotamia from her body, the twin rivers Tigris and Euphrates flowing from her eyes. In the centre he created the great city of Babylon, with its palaces and temples, forming humankind to serve as slaves of the gods here below, placing an earthly king over them as viceroy of the deity.

Here we see clearly how war in heaven led step by step to human society and the human social order on earth. It gave legitimacy to rulers and peoples who saw themselves under the patronage of the righteous, victorious side in that primordial conflict. When an emergent cosmos begins to move from the oneness of primordial chaos or a single divine essence into a plurality of gods, angels and other entities, strife is likely to occur. The confrontation involves not only individual gods and goddesses, but also their attendant legions, celestial and terrestrial.

These forces in turn are linked to warring tribes and kingdoms here below, each perhaps favoured by particular divinities as were the Greeks and Trojans or their heroes in the *Iliad*, even as those human battalions see in their ranks reflections of the swordsmen of the first days of creation. Inevitably, human communities take themselves to be heirs of the side regarded as aligned with cosmic justice in those transcendent conflicts, and the sacred centre of the community may well be the bastion of that deity, like the temple of Marduk in Babylon, called the 'House which is the Foundation of Heaven and Earth'.

Although war has no part in the creation story of Judaism and Christianity, the sacred city Jerusalem is a counterpart to 'Babel' or Babylon as a focus of divine meaning on earth. The City of David was not only the place where many sacred events occurred, but a timeless symbol of God's presence and activity.[123] Thus: 'The Lord loveth the gates of Zion [the hill in Jerusalem on which the Temple was built] more than all the dwellings of Jacob.' (Ps. 87: 2) 'Our feet shall stand within thy gates, O Jerusalem.' (Ps. 122: 2) 'I will rejoice in Jerusalem, and joy in my people: and the voice of weeping shall be no more heard in her, nor the voice of crying.' (Isa. 65: 19) Jerusalem was even a centre of the opposite of war:

> For the law shall go forth of Zion, and the word of the Lord from Jerusalem,
> and he shall judge among many people, and rebuke strong nations afar off;
> and they shall beat their swords into plowshares,
> and their spears into pruninghooks:
> nation shall not lift up a sword against nation,
> neither shall they learn war any more. (Micah 4: 2–3)

And finally: 'I John saw the holy city, new Jerusalem, coming down from God out of heaven.' (Rev. 21: 2)

War Defines Communities

So it is that nonetheless war, or at least warlike preparations and symbols, such as the brandished weapons found on numerous heraldic emblems, including the Great Seal of the United States, help define a sacred area, and a special or sacred people: Shambhala, Babylon, Jerusalem, and they that dwelt therein, together with other folk more recent. That land or city, its people and its symbols, so closely define 'who we are' to devotees of its gods, that they are prepared to defend its holy ground through violence unto death if need be. Not a few traditional societies see themselves as a distinct unit, whether village, tribe or folk, with their own particular myths of creation and legitimacy. Over against this people the outside world represents the 'other'. Almost by definition the foreign otherness is seen as chaotic, and against it continual vigilance, if not war, is a natural state.

The nineteenth-century philosopher F. W. J. Schelling, in his *Philosophy of Mythology*, wrote that 'A people exists as such only after defining itself and making its decision in its mythology.' To have one's own myth is the key to separateness: mythology arises in 'the transitional stage, when a people has not yet defined itself but is in the process of separating and closing itself off from mankind'. It is at that point mythology is no doubt especially potent and creative, though certainly so long as that people or nation sees itself as distinct from others, the mythology remains as a 'legacy' or even an inspiration, and all too often becomes a part of the ideology of war.[124]

Of the Anggor in western New Guinea, Peter Birkett Huber wrote, each village 'can be considered a cosmos in itself, an autonomous and essentially harmonious moral system confronted by a uniformly hostile, dangerous and chaotic outside world. Violence between these villages is consequently not a form of policy or a distinct kind of political situation, but an inescapable feature of man's existential condition.'[125] Most warfare between these villages is conducted by sorcery, but on occasion armed expeditions set forth to engage the 'other' by means of physical violence. Anggor warriors then, in the words of Bruce Lincoln, 'venture from their homes to confront chaos itself and, by means of this confrontation, reassert the solidarity of their group and the order of their cosmos by inflicting retaliatory deaths on their enemies outside.'[126] Huber concluded, in subsequent discussion his paper, that Anggor don't see violence as an extension of policy, or as a technique of social control, but

> They respond to violence as a threat by closing ranks and affirming commitments with the village. This involves a paradox because in the very act of opposing outsiders and denying relationships with them one affirms one's relationship with one's own kinsmen. The whole idea of kinsmen as opposed to strangers grows out of this experience of constant tension between the villages.[127]

Along with these insights must be added the way in which the enemy 'other' is almost inevitably dehumanized amid the high-decibel rhetoric of war, perhaps as a natural consequence of closing ranks and reaffirming one's own kinship ties in the act of opposing 'strangers', though they be just of the next tribe. Hostile people are not fully human, but caricatured as bestial or demonic, called dogs, vermin, trash or worse, and often bearers of demeaning nicknames. In the twentieth century, Germans were 'Huns', Japanese 'Nips', other Asians 'Slopes' or 'Gooks'.[128] Consider again how in that great modern cinematic myth, *Star Wars*, the troops on the imperial side were robot-like beings, faceless, identical, all male; or uniformed officers; or Darth Vader himself, also faceless and more machine than man. In contrast, in the valiant Rebel Alliance appears a diversity of faces, species, gender and personality, working together – sometimes quarrelling – as free beings, not automatons or slaves.[129]

War and the Initiation of the Warrior

A crucially important aspect of war and mythology is the initiation of warriors into their role. Potential warriors may be born, and in that oldest and arguably still greatest literary picture of what it means to be a warrior, the Iliad of Homer, we find that a combatant as mighty as Achilles was born of divine and human parentage, as was that strongest of champions, Hercules. Thus they may be said to have been born to prowess in feats of arms.

Others, however, require careful training to become a fighting-man. That education is not only in the technical skills of war, from swordsmanship to the piloting of warplanes, but also in crucial attitudes of mind and emotion, so different from those suited to days of peace. The soldier must, ideally, be able to act out of instant intuition, kill without qualms, remain unflinching in the face of mortal danger and obey orders without question. In other words, his training, like any effective initiation, changes him into a new person, emotionally, even physically, as well as intellectually. He is partly dehumanized from what he was before, if by that one means the rumpled, slouching, self-indulgent civilian of military caricature, but all the better able to do the work of a warrior directly, efficiently and without unnecessary reflection. One important component of such an initiation is placing the initiate firmly in a lineage sanctified by myth central to his culture, in which his role is modelled, idealized and made crucially important to both heaven and earth.

The medieval knight of western Europe – mythic heir, as we have seen, of St Michael and Wotan – was therefore created in a dubbing ceremony sometimes even called ordination, like that of a cleric. The rite was usually held on a holy day, such as Easter or Whitsunday. The candidate would confess his sins to a priest, take a purifying bath and dress in white linen. He would be expected to keep vigil in a chapel through the night, meditating on the vows of chivalry he was about to assume. In the morning, as mass was being said, every part of his armour would be blessed and anointed with holy oil before he solemnly put it on. Finally, in his actual 'dubbing' as a knight, the squire would be struck a sharp blow on the cheek by his king or feudal lord, to remind him of the pain he might suffer for his calling. He would then be 'sent forth', sometimes literally mounting his horse and attacking a black dummy representing an infidel enemy on his way out.

The knight would, of course, be expected to follow the code of chivalry, meaning he would fight only for a just cause, defending women and the innocent, following an honourable life. But as for killing, none other than St Bernard, writing on behalf of the Knights Templars, that great religious order of knights, affirmed that, 'The soldiers of Christ can fight the Lord's battles in all safety. For whether they kill the enemy or die themselves, they need fear nothing. To die for Christ and to kill his enemies, there is no crime in that, only glory.'[130]

The training of warriors today in such countries as the United States typically represents no less of an initiation. During the three months or so of 'boot camp', the initial and most intense period of transformation from civilian to soldier, recruits are isolated from all but very minimal outside contact, even from family, and subjected to a highly rigorous life in company with fellow-recruits from morning to night, of marching, intense physical activity, and obedience. Extreme fatigue combined with loud abuse or punishment for any infraction does much to produce the new personality: one self-aware, disciplined down to control of the slightest sound or movement, immediately responsive to situations and orders (however brutal they may be), bonded to the trooper's comrades and unit. In some tribal cultures, like that of the Native American Crow or the New Guinea Koko, young men were expected to have killed a man in combat before they could themselves be considered fully initiated as warriors, take their place in adult male society, perhaps even before they could marry the daughter of another proud warrior.

War and Sacrifice

In a previous chapter we have examined sacrifice, the 'making sacred' of something or someone through the offering, often by death, of that being to the divine. Killing and being killed in war, when that warfare is itself seen as in some way sacred, is surely not far removed from sacrifice generally in concept, and the connection is very often made.

We may first take a particularly grim example: Hitler's 'war against the Jews', victims whose deaths are in fact now commonly spoken of as the Holocaust (Shoah), in the Hebrew scriptures a sacrifice completely consumed by fire. From another perspective, Princess Marie Bonaparte, friend and wealthy patron of Freud and Freudians, herself a psychoanalyst, in an unusual little book, *Myths of War*, compared that Holocaust to the blood offered the Aztec war god Huitzlipochtli. This descendant of Napoleon further wrote, 'The atrocities of the Nazi concentration camps cannot be understood unless they are seen in their true light as acts of faith, auto-da-fés.'[131] Those terrible deaths, which only became more numerous as the Third Reich's inevitable defeat drew nearer and nearer, were like increasingly frantic offerings to dreadful Nazi gods who might, if sufficiently appeased, somehow still avert the end their devotees saw coming. Of course they did not, but something was fanatic, even religious, in the diabolical effort.

On the other hand, we speak of those who have died in a war considered good as having made 'the supreme sacrifice', and give them corresponding praise; and that which is sacrificed is made holy, made glorified and glorious. Countless uses of these words in connection with war dead could be adduced. Here are a few lines from a World War I poem by Walter de la Mare:

> Bitterly England, must thou grieve –
> Though none of these poor men who died
> But did within his soul believe
> That death for thee was glorified.[132]

Terrorism

Of particular concern today is what is called 'terrorism': the indiscriminate destruction of 'enemy' life and property by underground groups, with a view to expressing rage and so demoralize the foe as to win concessions, and make his defeat easier. Terrorism is often exercised by groups professing to be acting in the name of religion, most frequently a 'fundamentalist' version of the faith.

Terry Eagleton, in an interesting analysis of the situation, has pointed out that the fundamentalist, of whatever creed, believes 'that nothing has meaning or value unless it is founded on cast-iron principles'.[133] For a convinced believer of this stamp, absolute truth and nihilism – 'nothing is true' – are at opposite poles, no gray in between. To such a mind, the social correlate of nihilism is anarchy, lawless social chaos; even as that of absolute truth is a perfectly ordered social order. But, with help, the two opposites can easily flip from one to the other; they have a secret kinship in that they are both absolute, a quality the terrorist understands, though he hates and cannot accept contingency or ambivalence.

So it is that, by terrorism's particular style of logic, the creation of nihilism and anarchy invites in the coming kingdom of pure belief and the perfect society. This is the same logic as that of apocalyptic: only after conditions have gotten as terrible as conceivable, maybe moving even into the realm of the inconceivable, then in a single, sudden, unimaginably wondrous reversal the kingdom of God breaks through. The secular gospel of revolution, powerful throughout the world over the two centuries 1789–1989, from the French Revolution to the collapse of its last major ideological advocate, Soviet Communism, essentially declared the same vision: by speeding up progress to the work of a single mighty blow, the old is destroyed and, in its place, a new world arises pure and pristine. For those unable to mount a full-scale revolution, terrorism can attempt the same job piece-work.

The Joy of War

Finally, in yet another twist in the mystery of war, let us note for all the pain and tears; war has also been regarded as intensely joyous, affording a level of meaning and rapture rarely felt otherwise. General Pershing, in 1916, quashing an Army study on the causes of war, said the answer was obvious: 'Men go to war because they enjoy it.'[134] Beyond doubt, though they might deny it, not a few feel much more alive, even much happier, amid the tumult and excitement of war than in ordinary conditions. Lawrence LeShan, in *The Psychology of War*, relates that issue directly to our study by saying the joy of war wells up deep within us because battle enables to move into what he calls 'mythic' as opposed to 'sensory' reality, the twain may also be called wartime versus peacetime perceptions of the world and our role in it.[135]

Much is profoundly satisfying and exhilarating about the mythic wartime mode of being. The grey ambiguities of most human issues, the tedium of everyday, the inner sense of meaninglessness about so much of what we feel and do, are washed away and replaced by a world of brilliant colours, of stark contrasts because good and evil, and between us and them. In wartime, one's days and actions, however hard, are swept up into a great cause and dedicated to an overwhelmingly important end. Martin Van Creveld does not hesitate to compare the intensity of war to sexual excitement, and to observe – as a whole underground of suggestive quotes and cartoons bear witness – that for many men killing an enemy strangely resembles discharging one's seed sexually.[136]

Moral issues too are simplified – whatever advances the cause, even murder, is justified. In war, problems can be resolved – in our mythic fantasies – as if magically by swift, decisive and violent strokes. Furthermore, the war or revolution promises, again virtually like religious apocalyptic, that once the struggle and the sacrifices are over, the hours of ghastly fear gone and the demonic enemy vanquished, victory will bring days of superabundant peace and plenty.

LeShan quotes a person recalling the experience of living through the Blitz in London:

> A wretched time people say. I recall it as one of the happiest periods of my life. Living became a matter of the next meal, the next drink. The way people behaved to each other relaxed strangely. Barriers of class and circumstances relaxed ... the sense of two 'real' worlds, openly repressive and egalitarian, struggling with each other, was exhilarating.[137]

In conclusion, LeShan states:

> [T]he promise of war offers a clean conscience, full membership in a group, meaningfulness to one's actions and intensity in one's life, and a chance to change to an easier, less stressful, more magical way of organizing reality. Where else can you get all that at once?[138]

Another writer, Chris Hedges in *War Is a Force that Gives Us Meaning*, imparts a similar message. For him, war is like an addiction. He himself, as a reporter often covering war zones for the *New York Times*, felt its pull even as he was also repelled by its horror. He found himself returning time and again to war, always seeking out the heart of what was going on. He explained it in this way:

> The enduring attraction of war is this: Even with its destruction and carnage it can give us what we long for in life. It can give us purpose, meaning, a reason for living. Only when we are in the midst of conflict does the shallowness and vapidness of much of our lives become apparent. Trivia dominates our conversations and increasingly our airwaves. And war is an enticing elixir. It gives us resolve, a cause. It allows us to be noble.[139]

One is reminded of the comment of Joseph Campbell, a figure often cited in these pages, and who would certainly understand that myth, and living mythically, would help us realize the experience of which he speaks, to the effect that

> People say that what we're all seeking is a meaning for life. I don't think that's what we're really seeking. I think that what we're seeking is an experience of being alive, so that our life experiences on the purely physical plane will have resonances within our own

innermost being and reality, so that we actually feel the rapture of being alive. That's what it's all finally about, and that's what these clues help us to find within ourselves.[140]

Needless to say, many do not respond to war in this way. Some civilians in any war are never convinced of its joy even if they buy into its grim necessity; for others the war loses its glamour as soon as the first enthusiasm wears off, and the shortages and casualties begin to build up. By then it may be too late to back out.

Nor is war always experienced in that intensely joyous way by soldiers in the front lines day after day. For them, as LeShan and Hedges, like Jünger, make clear, the nobility is swallowed up by sickening fear, hatred of the enemy, and often hatred of oneself at what one is doing. What keeps troops going, as every experienced soldier knows, is not the myths but the profound bonding, closer than love, of comrades in a fighting unit. They keep at it because they cannot let one another down, and often they do not want to talk about it later, though it may recur in dreadful dreams. It is rather the occasional participant, the home front, and – when not too cynical – the leadership that gains much of the meaning of living in the time of war. Yet at the same time, living in war is an experience of living in a world of myth and mythic meaning as powerful as any available in the world today. It goes without saying that, until the deep, often subconscious, human needs that are met by war are fully addressed, war is unlikely to go away as a human activity no matter how many treaties and peace conferences we have.

Chapter 14

The End of Days

After the Sun Is Darkened

For planet earth as we have known it, the sands of time are running out. The world is seized with unprecedented wars and rumours of war as nation rises against nation, and along with these tribulations famine and earthquakes. Followers of Jesus are delivered up to those who would put them to death. Many flee, hardly knowing where to go, and whispers of false messiahs here or there buzz from mouth to mouth. Then dawns a day which is not really a day, for the sun rises black, and the following night falls darker still, for the moon gives no light, and stars drop from heaven as the power of the cosmos itself is shaken.

Then, when it seems the situation could get no worse, a trumpet blast is heard. From one end of the world to the other supernatural light sweeps across the sky, and in its central glory reigns the Son of Man, he who had once been despised and rejected of men, now luminous as a stained-glass window. The scars of nail and thorn puncture still his hands and brow. But now he is enthroned amid the radiance of eternity in simple but solemn splendour, as rightful king of all below, his haloed disciples at his side, the surrounding air alive with adoring angels.[141]

All humankind, the living and the far more numerous dead, the latter resurrected from soil or sea in new bodies, stand before him awaiting pronouncement of their eternal fate. The most powerful and poignant account of that dread moment is that of Matthew 25. This wonderful parable relates that the supreme judge will separate the peoples one from another as a shepherd separates the sheep from the goats, and will say to the sheep at his right hand, 'Come, O blessed of my Father, inherit the kingdom prepared for you from the foundation of the world; for I was hungry and you gave me food, I was thirsty and you gave me drink, I was a stranger and you welcomed me, I was naked and you clothed me, I was sick and you visited me, I was in prison and you came to me.' When they asked when they did these things, he will reply, 'Truly, I say to you, as you did it to one of the least of these my brethren, you did it to me.' But to the others he will say, 'As you did it not to one of the least of these, you did it not to me', and they will go away into eternal punishment, even as the righteous proceed rejoicing into eternal life.

Lord of the Dance

A picture from further east tells of Shiva, the great Hindu god who is Nataraja, Lord of the Dance. Throughout each *kalpa* or age of the world, equal to over four billion earth years, he progresses through his repertoire of dances, 108 in all. They resonate with the many moods of cosmic and historical time, some fast and energetic, some graceful and slow, reflecting all the permutations of life and love on earth. But finally, when the concert draws to a close, and it would be time for the performer to appear before the curtains to receive applause, this Dancing Lord begins beating his drum louder and louder, until the vibrations shatter the fabric of the world, and all is reduced back to primordial chaos.

That is no ultimate conclusion, however, for the Hindu creation and destruction of the universe is cyclical, a new spring following each dead winter. In due course, after he has sufficiently rested, the dancer will again take up his drum and, beginning perhaps with light tentative taps, then more and more assertive sounds and steps, the world-story commences again, possibly with a few variations, and so over and over into infinite future, for this is a dance with periods of respite, but with no beginning or end.

Eschatology and the Axial Age

The study of the end of time is called eschatology, and it is an important branch of religion and mythology. Eschatology often means the defeat of evil. Here at the end the saviour's inner victory becomes manifest outwardly: the evil world is cleansed or destroyed, and good triumphs, in those traditions which point towards a final culmination.

This view includes myths of the flood, typically an early example of world-cleansing that is like a foretaste of the End. Stories of universal or quasi-universal floods by which the world – or a part of it, like Atlantis – was cleansed of evil in order to make a new start are remarkably common. They are found in cultures from biblical to Greek, Chinese and American. Even though the watery defeat of evil is never permanent, the significance of world-washing tales should be understood. Flood myths project a revealing view of the gods who order the deluge, present concretely the archetypal meaning of water itself, and highlight the crucial importance of that small number of humans who are allowed to survive in order to perpetuate the race: Noah, Utnapishtim, Deucalion.[142]

The Last Days of apocalyptic make ultimate the purification foreshadowed in the flood. Even those creeds with a cyclical view of time, such as Hinduism, Buddhism and Platonism in the West, postulate the conclusion of one cycle and the inauguration of a new world-dance in dramas comparable to once-for-all eschatology, as we saw in the case of Shiva. Like many other points of religious and philosophical belief, different views of the apocalypse and the afterlife depend on what questions are being asked in a given culture and historical period. These queries in turn, as the philosopher Susanne Langer has pointed out, are shaped by ever-changing horizons of knowledge and experience.[143]

The most decisive occasion to raise new questions and stimulate new views of the afterlife and end-times was undoubtedly the discovery of history, that is, the realization that we live in linear, historical time. Events happen, times change, and do not change back to what they were before. The world is not cyclical, at least in the short term, but an ongoing irreversible process, and towards what final consummation it is headed is not immediately apparent.

The 'discovery of history' is no doubt closely connected to the invention of writing. Only then could chronicles be kept which showed that change is ongoing, without pause for breath or repetition. This discovery incited what is called the Axial Age, the time around the fifth century BCE which wrought tremendous change in the spiritual and intellectual life of much of the world, including the rise of the great religions started by known historical founders: Buddhism, Confucianism, later Christianity and Islam, as well as of the Hinduism centred on such deities as Shiva.

The great new question, then, was 'How do we deal with historical time, which so easily appears to be little more than one bad thing after another? How can we know if it is ultimately in good hands, or God's hands?' The answer was, first, the appearance in the midst of history of a transcendent teacher or saviour able to see beyond the tangles of time, and show a way of understanding and exit. In the words of the famous Christmas hymn about Bethlehem and the birth of Jesus: 'The hopes and fears of all the years are met in thee tonight.'

The second answer, then, was the vision of a glorious ending to the oft-dismal course of history, a culminating point at which that teacher may himself return, wipe away all tears, and make it all justified.

The teacher may propound a mystical state in which the temporal river ceases its flow to become calm to inward experience, or teach how to make ritual sacred worlds outside the circles of ordinary space and time. Most important for us now, though, are the Axial Age's renewed emphases on individual afterlife based on personal merit, and on the coming of a Last Day when all tears will be wiped away and the meaning of history, with all its suffering and seeming defeat of the good, will be made clear. This chapter began with a Christian apocalyptic scenario laden with such meaning.

It is appropriate, then, to end a discussion of the mythology of evil with that Day of Days.

Day Here, Night There

In primal societies, before the discovery of history, the question was not about the long-term destiny of the world, for as Mircea Eliade has argued in *The Myth of the Eternal Return* (1954), in those ancient days every year essentially repeated the original creation. Time was renewable, ever fresh, mythologically and ritually speaking. Death then was a process which merely enabled one to repeat the drama of life again, either in this world or another probably very like ours. Moreover, although one's ritual status could make a difference, individual judgement was frequently not viewed as seriously as later in a broad sense members of a family or tribe all enjoyed the next life together as they did this one. Indeed, ancestral spirits sharing one's home and village could be a powerful force in life. The key questions were not only what can we know about the afterlife, but also how can we maintain good relationships with those who have passed into it.

The earliest evidence of human afterlife belief is from burials, some as old as 40,000 years ago. Often the deceased was placed in a fetal position, suggesting return to the womb for rebirth, and smeared with red ochre, the colour of blood and so of life. Sometimes flowers were also placed in a tomb. It has been argued that the origin of religion was in shamanism, and the shaman's trance utterances have often been of communications from the departed. Recent theories have also suggested that the famous cave paintings were meant to record shamanistic visions and dreams.[144]

Quite often the Other World was conceived as being similar to this one, with its mountains, valleys, forests, villages comparable to those on this side. Among the Ainu of northern Japan, the other world is like ours but opposite, so that when it is day here it is night there and vice versa. Some say that souls rotate between the two, being born successively in one, then the other. For many of the Australian peoples, death means going to the Dreamtime, then returning to Spirit Wells to be reborn in this world.

The transition from this to the Afterlife realm, and one's status there, may entail meeting tests. Indeed, the journey of the soul can be compared to the hero's journey, with its call, its initiations, its road of trials, and its final reconciliation with the deities. In Malekula, an island in Vanuatu of Melanesian culture, a male soul had to pass a female monster named Lehevhev, who could be propitiated by the spirits of pigs sacrificed by the deceased in life. Those offerings were presented not only in public ceremonies, but also in men's secret lodges, where such oblations, especially of greatly-valued animals with double or triple curved tusks, could bestow higher and higher lodge degrees, and a correspondingly better world to come. It was said, however, that a man who had sacrificed even one such curved-tusk victim would be assured of an afterlife in a cool, pleasant land.[145]

In some early cultures, the realm of the dead is a gloomy prospect, far less inviting than this world. In a famous scene in Homer's Odyssey, the hero Odysseus goes to the underworld in order to consult the soul of Teiresias, a great seer, as to what he must do in order to return home. Odysseus was informed that first he had to sacrifice two sheep, for the departed are mere shades flitting mindlessly about until they take a sip of blood. A bit of that fluid of life will restore them long enough to speak to a mortal visitor. By this sanguinary means Odysseus converses not only with Teiresias, but also with such former comrades in the Trojan War as Achilles and Agamemnon (whom he learns was murdered by his wife on his return home), and with his own mother. One can well understand Odysseus' eagerness to depart Persephone's dark and ghostly realm; of it Achilles goes so far as to say that he would rather be a poor man's slave in the land of the living than king over all the dead.

Afterlife and Eschatology in Islam

In the Axial Age founder religions, characteristically individual immortality, as if it were a carryover from before the discovery of history, and the End-of-Days solution to the problem of meaning in history, must both be present and somehow integrated. Christian apocalyptic, such as that already described, coexisting as it does with the well-known Christian beliefs in an individual afterlife in heaven or hell immediately after death, is an example. Another may be found in Islam. Like all monotheistic religions, Islam emphasizes a highly contrasted heaven and hell. The Prophet said, 'When we live, we dream, and when we die, we wake' – to our true eternal nature and eternal life. Yet there is also a Day of Days, the Day of Judgement, at the end of this world. First the heavens and hells.

Heaven or paradise is actually seven heavens, progressively further and further from the material world, so that the seventh is in the presence of the sun-like brightness of God as comprehended by mystic vision. The concept is probably derived from pre-kabbalistic Jewish 'chariot mysticism', which based visionary ascent through seven spheres on an upward journey like that of Elijah's chariot; it no doubt also lies behind the Prophet Muhammad's famous Night Journey, when he was taken from the site of the Temple in Jerusalem to the highest of the seven heavens.

At the same time, Paradise, at least on the ordinary level, is conceived as Islam under the image of a garden, lush and well-watered, as one might expect of a desert people all too familiar with hard and barren terrain. Al-Jannah, the Garden (the term also refers to the Garden of Eden) is enclosed, sheltered from storm, abundant with fruit, blest with coolness and rest. Heaven also provided its inhabitants with houris, female companions who are perpetual virgins. These maidens are taken by mystical writers to symbolize spiritual states of rapture.

Hell is generally portrayed in terms of fire, sometimes also of great pressure. Sophisticated Islamic writers, ancient and modern, view hell less in terms of divine punishment than as an image of the endless self-contradiction and chaos of a life in denial of God, the one Reality. The question as whether hell is eternal is left open, though classical theologians have tended to feel that one who was so chaotic and torn apart by contradictions within between perverse belief and actual reality would only deteriorate further into nothingness rather than come out whole and alive. Yet the possibility remains; there is a Hadith (reported saying of the Prophet) that 'He shall make men come out of hell after they have been burned and reduced to cinders.' And another Hadith says: 'There who have merited paradise will enter it; the damned will go to hell, God will then say; Let those leave hell whose hearts contain even the weight of a mustard seed of faith: Then they will be released, although they have already been burned to ashes, and plunged into the river of rain-water, or into the river of life; and immediately they will be revived.'[146]

Muslim teachers also offer the hopeful possibility of a limbo or purgatorial state for those who are not ready for paradise, but open to further purification after death. Although not mentioned in the Qur'an, theologians have taken some Hadith such as the foregoing to suggest the probability of an intermediate state, or at least a non-eternal purification in hell, for those who are able to receive it. By the same token, authorities say that children who die before the age of reason will be saved in paradise.

Above all, Islam teaches the presence of God, the all-consuming Reality without a second, everywhere: Whichever way one looks, there is the Face of God, says the Qur'an. But whether one receives it as the cool, calm or paradise or the fires of hell depends upon one's own inner state.

But then there is also the Day of Judgement, Yawm ad-Din, which can also mean the Day of Religion, and is also called the Day of Resurrection. This Day and the coming judgement are major themes throughout the Holy Qur'an. The famous opening says:

> In the Name of God, the Merciful, the Compassionate
> Praise belongs to God, the Lord of all Being,
>   the All-merciful, the All-compassionate,
>   the Master of the Day of Doom.[147]

and in Sura 82:

> When the sky is torn
> When the stars are scattered
> When the seas are poured forth
> When the tombs are burst open
> Then a soul will know what it has given and what it has held back.[148]

Islamic tradition describes several events that will mark the approach of the Last Days. Some of them are clearly carried over from Jewish and Christian eschatological lore. Chaos and disorder, symbolized by Gog and Magog, will first break through all barriers set before them by the Shari'ah, or divine law. The Mahdi, or 'rightly guided one', a heroic figure, will arrive to restore the world to a brief period of moral and spiritual clarity. But his reign will be followed by another counter-force, the Anti-Christ (in Arabic *al-Masih ad-Dajjal*, literally 'impostor messiah'), a great deceiver who promises true revelation but delivers only tribulation and the turning upside-down of the cosmic and world order. (It is said that this imposer is one-eyed, symbolizing that he has no depth-perception, so mixes up the momentary and the eternal, and confuses affliction and sin.)

His time is short, and in the midst of his work of dizzying disorientation God breaks through: the Yawm ad-Din. A trumpet sounds; the world is knocked flat. It sounds again; the dead rise from their graves and are reunited with their bodies. The parts of the body themselves testify concerning their owner's good and bad deeds; it is said no deed praiseworthy or blameworthy, though it be small as an atom, is overlooked. It is then that the righteous enter the paradisal garden, the unrighteous the destroying flames of hell.

Here again individual immortality and the general judgement of the Last Day can be fitted together, but it is evident these are two different themes with two agenda: the judgement and fate of an individual life; and the wrapping-up of history, with its good and bad figures, its doctrines and empires, who operate on a world scale. These world-moving players are even more sharply-drawn than before as the End approaches. It is as though, the end coming near, the real plot-line of history with all its turbulence and moral seesawing is revealed in bold relief in the drama's last act. Good and evil vie back and forth to the end.

Entering the Pure Land

Finally, we turn to strands in the Axial Age tradition, in which Last-Day eschatology is of little importance compared to individual immortality. In Jainism, for example, it is held that since the number of souls is infinite, however many are liberated out of this universe, an infinite number remains, and the world continues on the same. For many ordinary Christians, simple life after death, remembered at funerals, is probably a more practical belief than eschatology.

We might note as an example what is called Pure Land Buddhism. While there is an eschatological side to Buddhism, centred around the coming of Maitreya, the future Buddha, an important form of Buddhism in East Asia is Amidism or Pure Land. The basic belief is that a cosmic buddha called Amitabha (Amida in Japanese), having attained ultimate enlightenment, was surrounded by a vast aura of light. This realm, extending billions of miles in all directions, appears to the eyes of the faithful entering it as a 'Pure Land', a paradisal realm of inexpressible beauty – fabulous flowers, trees garlanded with networks of jewels, celestial music in the air.

Moreover, out of his great compassion, Amida had vowed that all who called upon his name in simple faith would be brought into this wondrous heaven after death. (The concept has been compared to the Protestant reformer Martin Luther's concept of justification by faith: what is ultimately important is not adding up good and bad deeds, but the inner disposition, one's inward openness to ultimate reality, that counts.)

So, it is the beliefs and myths about the end of the world as we know it, or of life continuing after our present journey from birth to death, counter the evil of this world by showing there is more to existence than those limited spheres. They are contained in circles much larger, infinitely larger, and in them evil and death are swallowed up in victory.

Chapter 15

Summing Up

The Many Causes of Evil

According to myth, evil is multi-causal, just as is most of what happens in this world. 'Chaos theory', so much discussed in the natural sciences, and increasingly in connection with such human phenomena of human as fluctuations in the stock market and even the vagaries of mind and memory, bespeaks as much. It does not actually say sheer chaos reigns, in the sense that randomness rules and no cause exists but chance. Rather, causes of what makes events from the weather to Wall Street happen as they do are almost infinitely complex; tiny, almost imperceptible movements can, under the right conditions, increase exponentially to force big results (the famous 'butterfly effect': can the movement of the wings of a butterfly in Brazil cause a tornado in Texas?). No human mind or even computer can gauge all the factors in a highly complex system step by step; what can be done is to look for the cycles and patterns which inevitably emerge, though they themselves may branch into sub-patterns as intricate, and as fascinating, as those in a fractal design. In chaos theory, that effect is often compared to a tree, whose branches divide, subdivide and subdivide again into smaller and smaller units from trunk to twig, though each reflects on its own scale features common to the whole.[149]

How about evil? Is not that usually the way it is with bad things, including bad decisions, in our lives? We may see fault in our own flaws, those of others, circumstances, even the weather, and these all conspire to make something happen. Little happenings become big, obscure events, like a chance meeting, suddenly loom large – or not. Chaos-complexity means, as we have often said before in this study, that our lives are like stories, not philosophical abstractions. Only a gifted novelist could portray a character even approaching the potpourri that is real life.

Myths of evil, taken together, can tell stories mirroring that intricate complexity in real human life. To be sure, most individual myths are likely to focus on just one cause, and that is the weakness of myth as a total guide to life. As we have seen, such mythical thinking can work immense harm through oversimplification and 'demonizing' one particular factor or adversary. One may even project the evil within oneself onto an external 'shadow', making oneself falsely pure and another polluted.

But putting the many myths of evil together makes for a spectrum covering the broad band of human responses to evil. Here are some of those responses we have found.

Evil seems like a morass of defilement all around us, so that everything appears blighted, bland, viscous to the touch, far less than it was meant to be; and this is no doubt due to some wrong act or even thought back in the past.

Evil is caused by evil people. Some people, call them witches or psychopaths, are just bad, and do harm in devious, terrifying ways.

Evil is due to causes greater than just the human species, or even this planet, which is caught up a cosmic war or demonic rebellion against the Good. Our world, indeed our own hearts and minds, is a battlefield in this great conflict, but it is more than just us; that is why there is evil in nature as well as humanity.

Evil is due to some seemingly small accident: a misunderstanding about a divine gift, the eating of a forbidden fruit, a toad who hopped too ambitiously and spilled a precious elixir. It's the little things, the things that had consequences no one could have imagined, that add up like the butterfly effect to ruin a beautiful world.

Along with God, there seems to be from the beginning his shadow-side, his trickster counterpart, who always seems to want to spoil a good but rather prosaic creation with his clever ideas for making it more interesting, or who sees occasion for some 'joke' that leaves no one else the better, and is likely to backfire on the trickster himself. But the good God and the mischievous trickster keep running into each other, just as they no doubt do in human nature.

Initiations, natural or intentional, can work much harm in themselves; some seem virtually sadistic in the way they cause people to suffer in order to remake them into the image of lodge brother or sister, a monk or a fighting-man. Moreover, they can form people who are so transformed they can kill with no compunction, like an animal or a robot.

Next that starring figure or myth, the hero, rides in on his prancing charger. And what would the hero be without his adversary, his dragon or evil wizard, to fight against? A case could practically be made that evil exists so that heroes – and in this war, all of us can be heroes inwardly – may overcome enemies and thereby become greater than we were.

Finally, a still more disturbing thought, suggested in the chapter on war but also adumbrated in the trickster and his peculiar sense of humour: we do evil because evil is fun. Something there is about rebellion, showing we are smarter than someone else by fooling them or cheating them even if the results devastate another's life, or something about the moral clarity we think we see in war, draws us in.

Put all these together, and we begin to have a map of the malevolent. First we ought to notice our own very ambivalent feelings about evil in the wide spectrum of emotional and intellectual feelings these mythic answers evoke. We begin to realize that myths of evil are actually not so much explanations of evil, even in what we may be pleased to call primitive, storybook form, as they are an inventory of varied ways of *feeling* about evil, of responding to it on other than purely rational terms. Second, we may go on to realize that, insofar as myths are stories held in common by a society, a religion, a prison population or some other particular human group, they are more than just an individual way of feeling about evil, but one shared by the group. Such a feeling-response is no doubt reinforced as the story is told over and over, proper feeling-responses being obviously approved by the group, and others winning frowns.

The shared story becomes part of the group charisma, what holds it together and perhaps draws people to it: 'I want to be like those who know what this story means.' When a myth functions like this, whether its content is intellectually sophisticated or not is less important than its social role. That is because what it really symbolizes is not some abstract truth, but the group itself. The 'truth' it conveys is the emotional life the group shares, and which holds it together.

Of What Use Is the Mythology of Evil?

To get at this question, let us consider again Ernst Jünger, with whose *Storm of Steel* we began the chapter on war. Throughout his life of over a century (1895–1998), Jünger had as ambiguous and controversial a relationship to Nazism and the German right as he did to war:

revulsion, fascination, attempts to escape either through travel or inward withdrawal. Particularly after the Second World War, during the 1950s, Jünger was taken with the allure of myth and the mythologizing of the world.[150] In 1957 he and Mircea Eliade, also cited in these pages, founded a well-regarded journal of the history of religion, *Antaios*.

It is interesting to note that Jünger and Eliade, together with such other figures associated with the mid-twentieth century revival of popular interest in myth as C. G. Jung and Joseph Campbell, have attracted controversy because of alleged connections with the political right and fascism. To sort the charges out requires careful individual attention and is beyond the scope of this book.[151] As we will see in the case of Jünger, the final verdict is again ambivalent; its resolution would require more insight into the total subjectivity of another person than is permitted most of us, though there is no question mistakes of judgement were made. What is of significance now, however, is the way the mid-twentieth century mythic revival associated with figures like Jung, Eliade, Campbell and Jünger, the promotion of the 'myth of myth' assertion that the understanding of myth could do much to help us with personal and world problems, was for many (not all) of its advocates associated with a reactionary stance towards the contemporary world. Mythologists like these seemed anti-modern, holding the modern world was fragmented and vitiated of the kind of meaning people of old saw in their world and lives; by recovering their myths we could recover something of that wisdom.

Yet, there is the healing side to knowing what myth is about as well. Ernst Jünger, though he had written conservative, nationalistic materials that the Nazis found useful, did not join the Party and in 1939 daringly published a novel, *On the Marble Cliffs*, which, though set in a highly dreamlike, mythical fantasyland, in its evocation of a disruptive, evil figure who came to power could be read as an anti-Nazi allegory.[152]

On 17 April 1945, in the last days of the war but still a Wehrmacht officer, Jünger wrote in his diary, while discussing the Book of Esther and the destiny of the Jews, 'It is impossible that such sacrifices [or such victims] should not give fruits', thus associating the Holocaust of the Jews with religious sacrifice, as did Princess Marie Bonaparte.[153] In a tract called *Der Friede* (Peace) which Jünger apparently circulated among fellow German officers in 1944, when the writer was on the fringes of the officers' plot to assassinate Hitler, he urged that peace must be attained immediately, without winners or losers (of course at this point that would have been to Germany's advantage), and would be based on the 'fruitful sacrifice' of all war dead, especially 'innocent' victims, among whom the Jews were often mentioned.[154]

So, it is the mythology that gives significance to death by elevating it to the level of sacrifice, making it understood – like so much of evil and heroism – in the context of ancient lore and cosmic meaning. Does it also diminish the unique individuality, the intensely personal tragedy, of each separate victim and his or her family? That only those who survive can decide. We mark many graves with religious symbols, including that great emblem of sacrifice, the cross. Ernst Jünger became more and more devoutly Christian after the Second World War.

Understanding Myth

Myth, in the sense of telling a cosmic story to explain what happens here in our world in the largest possible context, is one way to deal with evil, but only one. It raises many complex problems as it endeavours to deal with the problem of evil. Myth can present an overwhelmingly powerful narrative of cosmic battle or delusion, which imperatively invites hearers or readers to themselves join that sublime adventure on the side of right. Yet as we have seen, myth can tend to polarize matters in stark black and white, right versus wrong terms, that grossly oversimplify the way matters usually are in the real world, and encourage the 'demonization' of the other side as virtually non-human, or as error which has no rights.

At the same time, it is possible to mythologize a religious worldview to the extent that it is distanced as possible truth, and can be read merely as effective story-telling. This is no doubt often the case with John Milton's powerful interpretation of what he saw to be the basic Christian story of Satan's rebellion and the fall of Adam and Eve in *Paradise Lost*, a work of great drama and grand poetry, but which may have subtly served to move that tale from revelation to literature; so also perhaps the *Ramayana*.

We have also already alluded to another issue: the way in which preoccupation with myth can lead to a nostalgic idealization of the past out of which myth derived, and so in some cases to unbalanced anti-modern, reactionary cultural values and highly nationalistic politics, the latter especially in view of the nineteenth-century's quest for core national myths, such as those of King Arthur in England or the *Nibelungenlied* in Germany. Understandably, after the Second World

War mytho-political nationalism fell into some disfavour, though cultural anti-modernism seasoned by mythology retained life.[155] The principal adjustment, however, has been in the direction of what I have called the 'myth of myth' – the view, highly evident in the work of C. G. Jung and Joseph Campbell, that however dangerous myth may have become in the political arena, it retains intra-psychic value, as a way of helping people to understand and re-assess their own nature. It is often found therapeutic to look at oneself as though a mythic archetype, or rather balanced constellation of archetypes, and to see the adventure of one's life as like the hero's quest.

This may be legitimate, and certainly ancient myth was sometimes seen as individual models as well as communal. Yet Sophia Heller's argument, in *The Absence of Myth*, should be taken seriously. She asks, if myth is now given such a different meaning than anciently, is it still myth? Then, people would say, we do things such a way because our ancestors so did them, as recorded in our myths. To use the same myth merely to come to terms with one's own father is hardly the same thing, and anyone who believed most myths (except those embedded in living religions) too literally would be considered highly delusional.[156]

Yet, the mirror that myth holds up to human nature is likely to abide one way or another. For, as we have suggested, myth is really less about doctrine, whether religious, scientific or psychological, as about *feeling*: how do we *feel* about the cosmos or, in the present case, evil loose within it. Does it feel like archangels in rebellion, or a presumptuous toad? A polluting oil-slick or a dragon to test a hero's daring? All this myths can help us clarify, and in the process aid us realizing that evil, like the cosmos as a whole, is both objective and subjective, both out there and within ourselves.

Bibliography

Aho, James A., *Religious Mythology and the Art of War*. Westport, CT: Greenwood Press, 1981.

Aho, James A., *This Thing of Darkness: A Sociology of the Enemy*. Seattle, WA: University of Washington Press, 1994.

Awn, Peter J., *Satan's Tragedy and Redemption: Iblis in Sufi Psychology*. Leiden, the Netherlands: E. J. Brill, 1983.

Berkson, Carmel, *The Divine and Demonic: Mahisa's Heroic Struggle with Durga*. Delhi & New York: Oxford University Press, 1995.

Campbell, Joseph, *The Hero with a Thousand Faces*. New York: Bollengen Foundation, 1949.

Cole, Phillip, *The Myth of Evil: Demonizing the Enemy*. Edinburgh: Edinburgh University Press, 2006.

de Rougemont, Denis, *The Devil's Share*. New York: Pantheon, 1944.

Douglas, Mary, *Purity and Danger*. London: Routledge & Kegan Paul, 1966.

Dundes, Alan, ed., *The Flood Myth*. Berkeley, CA: University of California Press, 1988.

Eagleton, Terry, *Holy Terror*. Oxford: Oxford University Press, 2005.

Ellwood, Robert, *Myth: Key Concepts in Religion*. London and New York: Continuum, 2008.

Ellwood, Robert, *The Politics of Myth*. Albany, NY: State University of New York Press, 1999.

Fontenrose, Joseph, *Python: A Study of Delphic Myth and its Origins*. Berkeley, CA: University of California Press, 1959.

Frankfurter, David, *Evil Incarnate: Rumors of Demonic Conspiracy and Ritual Abuse in History*. Princeton, NJ: Princeton University Press, 2006.

Givens, R. Dale, and Nettleship, Martin A., eds, *Discussions on War and Human Aggression*. The Hague, the Netherlands: Mouton, 1976.

Heller, Sophia, *The Absence of Myth*. Albany, NY: State University of New York Press, 2006.

Hyde, Lewis, *Trickster Makes this World*. New York: Farrar, Straus and Giroux, 1998.

Bibliography

Iloanusi, Obiakoizu A., *Myths of the Creation of Men and the Origin of Death in Africa*. Frankfurt am Main: Peter Lang, 1984.

Jay, Nancy, *Throughout Your Generations Forever: Sacrifice, Religion, and Paternity*. Chicago: University of Chicago Press, 1992.

Johns, Andreas, *Baba Yaga: The Ambiguous Mother and Witch of Russian Folklore*. New York: Peter Lang, 2004.

LeShan, Lawrence, *The Psychology of War*. New York: Helios, 2002.

Levack, Brian, *The Witch Hunts in Early Modern Europe*. London & New York: Longman, 1987.

Lévi-Strauss, Claude, *The Raw and the Cooked*. New York: Harper & Row, 1969.

Lincoln, Bruce, *Death, War, and Sacrifice*. Chicago: University of Chicago Press, 1991.

Ling, Trevor, *Buddhism and the Mythology of Evil*. London: Allen & Unwin, 1962.

Losev, Alexei Fyodorovich, *The Dialectics of Myth*. Trans. Vladimir Marchenkov. London & New York: Routledge, 2003.

Medway, Gareth, *Lure of the Sinister*. New York: New York University Press, 2001.

Nettleship, Martin A., Givens, R. Dale and Nettleship, Anderson, eds, *War: Its Causes and Correlates*. The Hague, the Netherlands: Moutin, 1975.

O'Flaherty [Doniger], Wendy, *The Origins of Evil in Hindu Mythology*. Berkeley, CA: University of California Press, 1976.

Parkin, David, *The Anthropology of Evil*. Cambridge, MA & Oxford, UK: Basil Blackwell, 1985.

Ricoeur, Paul, *The Symbolism of Evil*. Boston: Beacon Press, 1967.

Russell, Jeffrey, *The Prince of Darkness: Radical Evil and the Power of Good in History*. Ithaca, NY: Cornell University Press, 1988. (See also other works by this author.)

Sandy, Peggy, *Fraternity Gang Rape: Sex, Brotherhood, and Privilege on Campus*. New York: New York University Press, 1990.

Scott, Niall, ed., *Monsters and the Monstrous: Myths and Metaphors of Enduring Evil*. Amsterdam, NY: Rodopi, 2007.

Steinberg, Jonny, *The Number*. Johannesburg & Cape Town: Jonathan Ball, 2004.

Stivers, Richard, *Evil in Modern Myth and Ritual*. Athens, GA: University of Georgia Press, 1982.

van Creveld, Martin, *The Culture of War*. New York: Ballantine Books, 2008.

Watts, Alan, *The Two Hands of God*. New York: George Braziller, 1963.

Widengren, Geo, *Mani and Manichaeism*. London: Weidenfeld & Nicolson, 1965

Zaehner, Robert C., *Zurvan: A Zoroastrian Dilemma*. Oxford: Clarendon Press, 1955.

Notes

*   In studies of African societies, the word 'witch' is commonly used to translate words for workers of evil magic regardless of gender, despite European usage; the difference between a 'witch' and a 'sorcerer' is that the former usually work in groups or 'covens', the 'sorcerer' as a solitary.
** Characteristic of the time in which it was written, 'man' in this passage should be taken to include both genders.
1. Peter Berger, *The Sacred Canopy*. Garden City, NY: Doubleday, 1969, p. 28.
2. C. S. Lewis, *The Voyage of the Dawn Treader* (1952), in *The Complete Chronicles of Narnia*. New York: HarperCollins, 2000, p. 358.
3. Dennis Tedlock, trans., *Popol Vuh* (revised edn). New York: Simon & Schuster, 1996, p. 73.
4. Paul Ricoeur, *The Symbolism of Evil*. Boston: Beacon Press, 1967, p. 18.
5. A. H. Krappe, *La génèse des mythes*. Paris: Payot, 1938. Cited in Susanne K. Langer, *Philosophy in the New Key* (3rd edn). Cambridge, MA: Harvard University Press, 1957, pp. 195, 197.
6. Summarized in Walter J. Ong, *Orality and Literacy: The Technologizing of the Word*. New York: Routledge, 1982, pp. 49–56. See Aleksandr Romanovich Luria, *Cognitive Development: Its Cultural and Social Foundations*. Trans. Martin Lopez-Morillas and Lynn Solotaroff. Cambridge, MA: Harvard University Press, 1976.
7. Walter J. Ong, *Orality and Literacy*, pp. 43–5.
8. See Mark Girouard, *The Return to Camelot*. New Haven and London: Yale University Press, 1981.
9. Sir Thomas Malory, *Le Morte D'Arthur* (1485). Edited by John Matthews. New York: Barnes and Noble, 2004, p. 70.

10 From Martha Asher, trans., *The Post-Vulgate, Part I: The Merlin Continuation*, in *Lancelot-Grail: The Old French Arthurian Vulgate and Post Vulgate in Translation*, 5 vols, New York: Garland, 1993–1996, IV, P. 214. Reproduced in Sir Thomas Malory, *Le Morte D'Arthur*. Ed. Stephen H. A. Shepherd. New York: W. W. Norton, 2004, p. 711.
11 Brannon Wheeler, *Mecca and Eden*. Chicago: University of Chicago Press, 2006, p. 129.
12 Paul Ricoeur, *The Symbolism of Evil*. Boston: Beacon Press, 1969, p. 25.
13 Ibid., p. 30.
14 Jane Austen, *Mansfield Park*. New York: W. W. Norton, 1998 (1st pub. 1814), p. 299.
15 Eurpides, *Orestes*. Trans. E. P. Coleridge (1910). Internet Sacred Text Archive, *The Dramas of Euripides*.
16 C. S. Lewis, *The Lion, the Witch and the Wardrobe*. New York: Scholastic, 1995 (1st pub. 1950), p. 59.
17 J. R. R. Tolkien, *The Return of the King* (2nd edn). Boston: Houghton Mifflin, 1965, p. 212.
18 From 'The City in the Sea', by Edgar Allan Poe.
19 Stephen Crane, *The Red Badge of Courage*. Pleasantville, NY: The Reader's Digest Association, 1982 (1st pub. 1895), pp. 44–5.
20 Jan Knappert, *Myths and Legends of the Congo*. London: Heinemann Educational Books, 1971, pp. 64–7.
21 Klaus E. Müller and Ute Ritz-Müller, *Soul of Africa: Magical Rites and Traditions*. Cologne, Germany: Könemann, 2000, p. 139.
22 Andreas Johns, *Baba Yaga: The Ambiguous Mother and Witch of the Russian Folktale*. New York: Peter Lang, 2004.
23 Linda J. Ivanits. *Russian Folk Belief*. Armonk, NY: M. E. Sharpe, 1989, pp. 95–6.
24 Brian Levack, *The Witch Hunt in Early Modern Europe*. London and New York: Longmans, 1987, p. 25.
25 David Bromley, *The Satanism Scare*. Piscataway, NJ: Aldine Transaction, 1991; Robert S. Hicks, *In Pursuit of Satan*. Buffalo, NY: Prometheus Books, 1991; Gareth J. Medway, *Lure of the Sinister*. New York: New York University Press, 2001; Jeffrey S. Victor, *Satanic Panic*. London: Open Court, 1993.
26 Mary Douglas, *Purity and Danger*. London and New York: Routledge, 2002 (Orig. pub. 1966), pp. 1–2.

27 Mary Douglas, *Natural Symbols*. New York: Vintage Books, 1973.
28 Sheldon R. Isenberg and Dennis E. Owen, 'Bodies, natural and contrived: The work of Mary Douglas', *Religious Studies Review* 3, no. 1 (January 1977), pp. 7–8. This article contains a useful chart of grid and group attitudes compared.
29 Raphael Falco, *Charisma and Myth*. London: Continuum, 2009.
30 See, for example, Martin L. Bowles, 'Myth, meaning and work organization', *Organization Studies* 1989, 10/3, pp. 405–21.
31 Denis de Rougemont, *The Devil's Share*. Trans. Haakon Chevalier. New York: Pantheon Books, 1944, pp. 62, 64.
32 Anthony S. Mircatante and James R. Dow, *World Mythology and Legend* (2nd edn). New York: Facts on File, 2004, vol. 1, p. 444.
33 Cyril Glassé, *The New Encyclopedia of Islam*. Walnut Creek, CA: AltaMira, 2001, p. 190.
34 Peter Lamborn Wilson, *Sacred Drift: Essays on the Margins of Islam*. San Francisco: City Lights Books, 1993, p. 88.
35 Two recent introductory books on Gnosticism that can be recommended are Stephan A. Hoeller, *Gnosticism: New Light on the Ancient Tradition of Inner Knowing*. Wheaton, IL: Quest Books, 2002; and Elaine Pagels, *The Gnostic Gospels*. New York: Random House, 1978. Like many contemporary presenters of Gnosticism, both discuss parallels, behind the often strange-sounding Gnostic myths, between the inner meaning of the ancient faith and modern existentialism, feminism and psychology, especially Jungian. See also Willis Barnstone and Marvin Meyer, eds, *The Gnostic Bible*. Boston & London: Shambhala, 2003, for translations of original Gnostic texts.
36 H. P. Lovecraft, 'The Haunter of the Dark', in S. T. Joshi, ed., *The Dunwich Horror and Others*. Sauk City, WI: Arkham House, 1984, p. 110.
37 Gavin Baddeley, *Goth Chic* (2nd edn). Medford, NJ: Plexus Publishing, 2006.
38 Claude Lévi-Strauss, *The Raw and the Cooked*. Trans. John Weightman and Doreen Weightman. New York: Harper, 1969.
39 Dennis Tedlock, trans., *Popol Vuh* (revised edn). New York: Simon & Schuster, 1996.
40 Alexander Heidel, *The Babylonian Genesis: The Story of Creation*. Chicago, IL: University of Chicago Press, 1963.
41 Hesiod, *Theogony and Works and Days*. Trans. Stanley

Lombardo and Robert Lamberton. Indianapolis, IN: Hackett, 1993.
42 Barbara C. Sproul, *Primal Myths*. HarperSanFrancisco, 1991, pp. 350–2.
43 Obiakoizu A, Iloanusi, *Myths of the Creation of Men and the Origin of Death in Africa*. Peter Lang: Frankfurt am Main, 1984, pp. 129–32.
44 Cornelia Dimmitt and J. A. B. van Buitenen, trans., *Classical Hindu Mythology: A Reader in the Sanskrit Puranas*. Philadelphia: Temple University Press, 1978, pp. 30–1; David R. Kinsley, *Hinduism: A Cultural Perspective* (2nd edn). Englewood Cliffs, NJ: Prentice Hall, 1963, p. 63; A. L. Dallapiccola, *Hindu Myths*. London: British Museum Press, 2003, p. 19.
45 'Golden Mycenae', in Donald S. Fryer, *Songs and Sonnets Atlantean*. Sauk City, WI: Arkham House, 1971, p. 28.
46 R. C. Zaehner, *Zurvan: A Zoroastrian Dilemma*. Oxford: Clarendon Press, 1955.
47 Geo Widengren, *Mani and Manichaeism*. London: Weidenfeld and Nicolson, 1965.
48 Mircea Eliade, Le créateur et son 'ombre', *Eranos-Jahrbuch 1961*. Zurich: Rhein-Verlag, 1962, p. 211.
49 James G. Frazer, *The Belief in Immortality*. London: Macmillan, 1913, vol. 1, pp. 72–3, quoting A. J. Kruit.
50 Finnegan, Ruth, *Limba Stories and Story-Telling*. Oxford: Clarendon Press, 1967, p. 234–5.
51 Obiakoizu A. Iloanusi, *Myths of the Creation of Man and the Origin of Death in Africa*. Peter Lang: Frankfurt am Main, 1984, pp. 160–2.
52 Hesiod, *Theogony and Works and Days*. Trans. Stanley Lombardo and Robert Lamberton. Indianapolis, IN: Hackett, 1993, pp. 25–6.
53 Tony Allen, 'Confronting the Final Mystery', in Duncan Baird Publishers, ed., *The Great Themes: World Myth*. Amsterdam: Time-Life Books, 2000, p. 108.
54 Horatio Hale, 'Huron Folklore', *Journal of American Folklore*, 1888, pp. 175–83. Reprinted in Barbara C. Sproul, *Primal Myths*. HarperSanFrancisco, 1991, pp. 346–8.
55 John Mohawk, *The Iroquois Creation Story*. Buffalo, NY: Mohawk Publications, 2005; John Bierhorst, *The Woman Who Fell from the Sky: The Iroquois Story of Creation*. New York: Morrow, 1993.

56 Frank Waters, *The Book of the Hopi*. New York: Viking, 1963, pp. 12, 15. Compare Harold Courlander, *The Fourth World of the Hopis*. New York: Crown, 1971, pp. 17–18. It should be noted that, as with most myths in living oral tradition, many versions are extant of the Hopi creation story. Waters' *Book of the Hopi* has been severely criticized by ethnologists and Hopi themselves for its 'confabulation of fact and imagination': Peter M. Whiteley, *Rethinking Hopi Ethnography*. Washington & London: Smithsonian Institution Press, 1998, p. 12, with references.
57 Friedrich Nietzsche, *The Birth of Tragedy and Other Writings*. Ed. Raymond Geuss and Ronald Spears. Trans. Ronald Spears. New York: Cambridge University Press, 1999.
58 C. Kerényi, *Dionysos: Archetypal Image of Indestructible Life*. Trans. Ralph Manheim. Bollenger series LXV: 2. Princeton, NJ: Princeton University Press, 1976. Walter F. Otto, *Dionysus: Myth and Cult*. Trans. Walter Palmer. Bloomington, IN: Indiana University Press, 1965. Richard Seaford, *Dionysos*. London: Routledge, 2006.
59 Otto, *Dionysus*, p. 142.
60 H. R. Ellis Davidson, *Scandinavian Mythology*. New York: Peter Bedrick, 1986, pp. 45–6, 101, 104.
61 Zora Neale Hurston, *Dust Tracks on a Road*. Philadelphia, PA: Lippincott, 1942, p. 95.
62 Zora Neale Hurston, *Mules and Men*. New York: Harper & Row, 1990 (originally pub. 1935).
63 Mark Thompson, 'Children of Paradise: A Brief History of Queers', in Mark Thompson, ed., *Gay Spirit: Myth and Meaning*. New York: St Martin's Press, 1987, p. 49.
64 Lewis Hyde, 'Where Are the Women Tricksters?' in Jeanne Campbell Reesman, *Trickster Lives: Culture and Myth in American Fiction*. Athens, GA: University of Georgia Press, 2001, pp. 185–93.
65 Thomson, 'Children of Paradise', p. 52.
66 Sacvan Bercovitch, 'Deadpan Trickster: The American Humor of Huckleberry Finn', in Jeanne Campbell Reesman, *Trickster Lives: Culture and Myth in American Fiction*. Athens, GA: University of Georgia Press, 2001, p. 65.
67 Ricki Stefanie Tannen, *The Female Trickster: The Mask that Reveals*. London: Routledge, 2007, p. 7–9.
68 Robert D. Hare, *Without Conscience: The Disturbing World of*

the Psychopaths among Us. New York: Guildford Press, 1993; Martha Stout, *The Sociopath Next Door.* New York: Broadway, 2005.

69   James G. Frazer, *The Belief in Immortality.* London: Macmillan, 1913, I, pp. 250–4.

70   George Catlin, *O-Kee-Pa: A Religious Ceremony and Other Customs of the Mandans.* Ed. John G. Ewers. New Haven; Yale University Press, 1967. (This classic account by the famous painter and ethnographer of the Old West, George Catlin, was first published in 1867.) See also Benjamin Capps, *The Old West: The Indians.* Alexandria, VA: Time-Life Books, 1973, pp. 140, 144–9.

71   Rita M. Gross, 'Tribal religions: Aboriginal Australia', in Arvind Sharma, ed., *Women in World Religions.* Albany, NY: SUNY Press, 1987, p. 43.

72   Franz Boas, 'The Shuswap' (offprint). Cited Mircea Eliade, *Shamanism: Archaic Techniques of Ecstasy.* New York: Pantheon, 1964, p. 100.

73   C. W. Leadbeater, *The Masters and the Path.* Adyar, India: Theosophical Publishing House, 1965, p. 220.

74   St Ignatius of Antioch, Epistle to the Romans. Francis X. Glimm, Joseph M.-F. Marique, S. J., Gerald G. Walsh, S. J., trans., *The Apostolic Fathers.* New York: Christian Heritage, 1947, p. 110.

75   H. R. Ellis Davidson, *Gods and Myths of the Viking Age.* New York: Bell, 1981, p. 67, citing G. Dumézil.

76   Mircea Eliade, *Rites and Symbols of Initiation.* New York: Harper & Row, 1965, p. 84.

77   H. R. Ellis Davidson, *Scandinavian Mythology.* New York: Peter Bedrick, 1988, pp. 36–8.

78   Jonny Steinberg, *The Number.* Johannesburg & Cape Town: Jonathan Ball, 2004, p. 23.

79   Peggy Sandy, *Fraternity Gang Rape: Sex, Brotherhood, and Privilege on Campus.* New York University Press, 1990, pp. 152–3.

80   Swami Prabhavananda and Christopher Isherwood, trans., *The Song of God: Bhagavad Gita.* Hollywood, CA: Vedanta Press, 1944, 1987, p. 58.

81   Cornelia Dimmitt, 'Sītā: Mother Goddess and Śakti', in John Stratton Hawley and Donna Marie Wolff, *The Divine Consort: Radha and the Goddesses of India.* Berkeley, CA: Graduate Theological Union, 1982, p. 214.

82 Carmel Berkson, *The Divine and Demonic: Mahisa's Heroic Struggle with Durga*. Delhi & New York: Oxford University Press, 1995.
83 Samantha Riches, *St George: Hero, Martyr, and Myth*. Thrupp, UK: Sutton, 2000.
84 J. R. R. Tolkien, *The Fellowship of the Ring, Being the First Part of The Lord of the Rings* (2nd edn). Boston: Houghton Mifflin, 1965, p. 69.
85 Alexei Fyodorovich Losev, *The Dialectics of Myth*. Trans. Vladimir Marchenkov. London & New York: Routledge, 2003, pp. 182–3.
86 Ibid., p. 145, 149.
87 Paul Ricoeur, *The Symbolism of Evil*. Boston: Beacon Press, 1967, p. 5.
88 Richard Stoneman, *Alexander the Great: A Life in Legend*. New Haven; Yale University Press, 2008; Stoneman, *The Greek Alexander Romance*. London: Penguin Books, 1991.
89 Richard Stoneman, *Legends of Alexander the Great*. London: J. M. Dent, 1994, pp. 67–75.
90 Bronislaw Malinowski, *Magic, Science and Religion and Other Essays*, Boston: Beacon Press, 1948, p. 93.
91 See Dan Merkur, *Psychoanalytic Approaches to Myth: Freud and the Freudians*. New York & London: Routledge, 2005; Robert Eisner, *The Road to Daulis: Psychoanalysis, Psychology, and Classical Mythology*. Syracuse, NY: Syracuse University Press, 1987; and Patrick Mullahy, *Oedipus: Myth and Complex*. New York: Hermitage Press, 1952.
92 Merkur, *Psychoanalytic Approaches to Myth*, pp. 29–30.
93 Sigmund Freud, *Civilization and its Discontents*. Trans. Joan Riviere. London: Hogarth Press, 1939 (orig. German pub. 1930).
94 C. G. Jung, *The Archetypes and the Collective Unconsciousness. Collected Works of C. G. Jung*. Trans. R. F. C. Hull. New York: Bollengen Foundation, 1959. Since 1967 pub. by Princeton University Press. See also Robert Segal, ed., *Jung on Mythology*. Princeton University Press, 1998.
95 Isaiah Berlin, *Vico and Herder: Two Studies in the History of Ideas*. New York: Viking, 1976, presents and excellent introduction to this thinker.
96 Isaiah Berlin, *Vico and Herder: Two Studies in the History of Ideas*. London: Hogarth Press, 1976, pp. 193–4. See also Robert

Ergang, *Herder and the Foundations of German Nationalism*. New York: Columbia University Press, 1931, especially pp. 195–212, though the term 'folk literature', not myth, is used here.

97   Edward Allen Beach, *The Potencies of God(s): Schelling's Philosophy of Mythology*. Albany, NY: SUNY Press, 1994.
98   Robert S. Segal, *Joseph Campbell: An Introduction*. New York: Garland Publishing, 1987, p. 137.
99   Joseph Campbell, *Myths to Live By*. New York: Viking, 1972, p. 214.
100 For a fascinating study of the English case, see Mark Girouard, *The Return to Camelot: Chivalry and the English Gentleman*. New Haven, CT: Yale University Press, 1981.
101 See Luc Brisson, *Plato the Myth Maker*. Trans. Gerard Naddaf. Chicago, IL: University of Chicago Press, 1998.
102 Donald L. Philippi, trans., *Kojiki*. Tokyo: University of Tokyo Press, 1968, pp. 74–92; Lewis Hyde, *Trickster Makes This World*. New York: Farrar, Straus and Giroux, 1998, pp. 178–80; Robert Ellwood, 'A Japanese Mythic Trickster Figure: Susa-no-o', in William J. Hynes and William G. Doty, eds, *Mythical Trickster Figures*. Tuscaloosa, AL: University of Alabama Press, 1993, pp. 141–58.
103 Mircea Eliade, *A History of Religious Ideas*. Chicago, IL: University of Chicago Press, 1978, vol. 1, pp. 223–35.
104 Michael J. Harner, *The Jivaro: People of the Sacred Waterfall*. Garden City, NY: Doubleday, 1972, p. 147.
105 Nancy Jay, *Throughout Your Generations Forever: Sacrifice, Religion, and Paternity*. Chicago, IL: University of Chicago Press, 1992.
106 Marie Antoinette Czaplicka, *Aboriginal Siberia*. Oxford: Oxford University Press, 1914, p. 172.
107 Andreas Lommel, *Shamanism: The Beginnings of Art*. New York: McGraw-Hill, 1967, p. 49.
108 Mircea Eliade, *Shamanism: Archaic Techniques of Ecstasy*. New York: Bollengen Foundation, 1964, pp. 60–61. Based on Knud Rasmussen, *Intellectual Culture of the Iglulik Eskimo*, Copenhagen, 1930, p. 111ff.
109 Say Cited in Andreas Lommel, *Shamanism: The Beginnings of Art*. New York: McGraw-Hill, 1967, p. 151.
110 Yakut and Buryat reference, Lommel, *Shamanism*, pp. 56–7.
111 Apuleius, *The Transformations of Lucius, otherwise known as*

The Golden Ass. Trans. Robert Graves. New York: Farrar, Straus and Giroux, 1951, p. 263.
112 Ibid., p. 277.
113 Ibid., p. 280.
114 Daisetz Teitaro Suzuki, *The Training of the Zen Buddhist Monk.* New York: University Books, 1965 (original pub. Tokyo 1934), pp. 3–11. It should be added that most young men entering a monastery in this way are not prospective lifetime monks, but aspirants to the priesthood of a local Zen temple; they will study and practice at a monastery for some three years, then return to a temple living, most likely one hereditary in the family, and probably marry.
115 Donald L. Philippi, trans., *Kojiki.* Princeton University Press, 1969, pp. 232–52; A. G. Aston, *Nihongi.* Rutland, VT & Tokyo: Tuttle, 1972 (orig. pub. 1896), II, pp. 200–11. It should be noted that the *Kojiki* (712 CE and the oldest extant Japanese book), and the *Nihongi*, or *Nihonshoki* (720 CE), give many of the same stories of Yamato-takeru but differ dramatically in portraying his relationship to his father, the emperor Keiko; in the *Kojiki*, just one of many princes, he is hated by his father for his violent temperament, and sent on missions clearly expected to end in his death; but in the *Nihonshoki* he becomes crown prince and is a man of upright character; he and his parent are made to exemplify ideal Confucian sovereign-subject and father-son relationships. Our telling of Yamato-takeru's story draws from both accounts, but for the most part from the *Kojiki*.
116 C. P. Cavafy, *Selected Poems.* Trans. Edmund Keeley and Philip Sherrard. Princeton, NJ: Princeton University Press, 1972, p. 18.
117 Bimala Churn Law, *Mahavira: His Life and Teaching.* Kolkata, India: Maha Bodhi Book Agency, 2002 (orig. pub. London, 1937).
118 Ernst Jünger, *Storm of Steel.* Trans. Michael Hofmann. London: Penguin Classics, 2004, p. 93 (orig. German pub. 1920); later slightly revised.
119 Ibid., p. 232.
120 Ibid., p. 241.
121 Ibid., p. 281–2.
122 James A. Aho, *Religious Mythology and the Art of War.* Westport, CT: Greenwood Press, 1981, pp. 81. Source of quote not given.

123 See Mircea Eliade, *The Sacred and the Profane*. New York: Harcourt Brace Jovanovich, 1959, pp. 31–2, 60–1.
124 Cited in Ernst Benz, 'Theogony and the Transformation of Man in Freidrich Wilhelm Joseph Schelling', in Joseph Campbell, ed., *Man and Transformation: Papers from the Eranos Yearbooks XXX/5*. New York: Pantheon Books, 1964, p. 214.
125 Peter Birkett Huber, 'Defending the Cosmos: Violence and Social Order among the Anggor of New Guinea', in Martin A. Nettleship, R. Dale Givens, and Anderson Nettleship, eds, *War: Its Causes and Correlates*. The Hague, the Netherlands: Moutin, 1975, p. 620.
126 Bruce Lincoln, *Death, War, and Sacrifice*. Chicago, IL: University of Chicago Press, 1991, p. 143.
127 R. Dale Givens and Martin A. Nettleship, eds, *Discussions on War and Human Aggression*. The Hague, the Netherlands: Mouton, 1976, p. 174.
128 See James A. Aho, *This Thing of Darkness: A Sociology of the Enemy*. Seattle, WA: University of Washington Press, 1994. The title comes from a line from Shakespeare's *The Tempest* v.i: 'This thing of darkness I acknowledge mine.'
129 See Mary Henderson, *Star Wars: The Magic of Myth*. New York: Bantam Spectra, 1997.
130 Aho, *Religious Mythology and the Art of War*, pp. 81–4.
131 Marie Bonaparte, *Myths of War*. Trans. John Rodker. London: Imago, 1947, p. 156.
132 'How sleep the brave,' in Walter de la Mare, *The Fleeting and Other Poems*. New York: Alfred A. Knopf, 1933, p. 84.
133 Terry Eagleton, *Holy Terror*. Oxford, UK: Oxford University Press, 2005, p. 26.
134 Cited in Lawrence LeShan, *The Psychology of War*. New York: Helios Press, 2002, pp. 71–2.
135 LeShan, *Psychology of War*, op. cit.
136 Martin van Creveld, *The Culture of War*. New York: Ballantine Books, 2008, pp. 110–11. This book is highly recommended for many perceptive insights on war and its human meaning.
137 LeShan, *Psychology of War*, pp. 85–6.
138 Ibid., p. 160.
139 Chris Hedges, *War Is a Force That Gives Us Meaning*. New York: Public Affairs Press, 2002, p. 3.
140 Joseph Campbell, with Bill Moyers, *The Power of Myth*. New York: Doubleday, 1985, p. 5.

141 Based on Matt. 24, Mark 13, Luke 21 (Revised Standard Bible), and other traditional Christian sources.
142 See Robert Ellwood, *Myth: Key Concepts in Religion*. London & New York: Continuum, 2009, pp. 111–14.
143 Susanne K. Langer, *Philosophy in a New Key* (3rd edn). Cambridge, MA: Harvard University Press, 1957, pp. 3–6.
144 See John E, Pfeiffer, *The Creative Explosion: An Inquiry into the Origins of Art and Religion*. New York: Harper & Row, 1982, pp. 210–25; and David Lewis-Williams, *The Mind in the Cave*. London: Thames & Hudson, 2002.
145 A. Bernard Deacon, *Malekula: A Vanishing People in the New Hebrides*. London: Routledge, 1924.
146 Glassé, *New Encyclopedia of Islam*, pp. 129, 176.
147 A. J. Arberry, *The Koran Interpreted*. New York: Macmillan, 1955, I, p. 29.
148 Michael Sells, trans., *Approaching the Qur'an: The Early Revelations* (2nd edn). Ashland, OR: White Cloud Press, 1999, p. 52.
149 James Gleick, *Chaos: Making a New Science*. New York: Viking, 1987.
150 On Jünger, see Elliot Neaman, *A Dubious Past: Ernst Jünger and the Politics of Literature after Nazism*. Berkeley, CA: University of California Press, 1999; and Thomas Nevin, *Ernst Jünger and Germany: Into the Abyss, 1914–1945*. Durham, NC: Duke University Press, 1996; and, for a more critical perspective, Marcus Paul Bullock, *The Violent Eye: Ernst Jünger's Visions and Revisions on the European Right*. Detroit, MI: Wayne State University Press, 1992.
151 See Robert Ellwood, *The Politics of Myth: A Study of C. G. Jung, Mircea Eliade, and Joseph Campbell*. Albany, NY: State University of New York Press, 1999.
152 Ernst Jünger, *On the Marble Cliffs*. Trans. Stuart Hood. Harmondsworth, England & Baltimore: Penguin Books, 1970.
153 Cristiano Grottanelli, 'Fruitful death: Mircea Eliade and Ernst Jünger on human sacrifice, 1937–1945', Numen 52: 1 (2005), p. 136.
154 Ibid., p. 138.
155 See my *The Politics of Myth*.
156 Sophia Heller, *The Absence of Myth*. Albany, NY: SUNY Press, 2006, pp. 217–21.

Index

Adam and Eve 7, 30–1, 101, 103, 145
 in Islam 15, 32–3
African American lore 56–7
Ahura Mazda 31, 44
Ainu 135
Alexander the Great 83
Amida 140
Amon-Re 37
Amos (Bible) 13
apocalyptic 31, 134–5, 137
 and terrorism 138
 and war 129
Apollo 17–18, 51
 and Nietzsche 52
Apuleius 104–6
Arthur, King 9, 26–7, 90, 145
 and Carbonek 14–15, 27
 and Holy Grail 14–15, 109–10
Austen, Jane 16–17
Australian aborigines 28, 48, 136
Axial Age 133–5

Baba Yaga 21–2
Babylonia 38, 85
 kingship in 122
Balder 55–6
Batman 59–60
Beowulf 8, 110

Bercovitch, Sacvan 58
Berger, Peter 5
Berserkers 60, 85
 initiation of 66–7
Bhagavad Gita 73, 117
Bonaparte, Princess Marie 127–8
Buddha, the 78, 80, 110, 116–18
 in Pure Land 140
 in Zen 108
Buddhism 43, 134, 140
Bugandan Queen 48
Buryat shamans 105

Cain and Abel 16
 sacrifices of 100–1
'Calamity Jane' 59
Campbell, Joseph 75, 89, 130, 144, 146
Cavafy, C. P. 114
Celebes 46, 96
chaos theory 141
Christianity 25, 31, 71
 creation account in 101, 123
 and 'Satanic Panic' 24
Congo 20
Coyote, as trickster 53–5, 58, 60, 97
 in shamanism 104
Crane, Stephan 18–19, 120
Creveld, Martin van 129
Czaplicka, Marie 104

Index

de la Mare, Walter 128
Dionysos 51–2
Dogon 41–2
Douglas, Mary 24–5
Durga 74–5

Eagleton, Terry 128
Eden 16, 30, 48, 97, 101
  in Islam 15, 32, 137
Eliade, Mircea 44–5, 54, 85, 135, 144
Enuma Elish 38
eschatology 133–5
  in Islam 137–9
  in Pure Land Buddhism 140
Eskimo (Inuit) 104–5
Euhemerism 83–4
Euripedes 17
evil, meaning of 4–5

Falco, Raphael 26
Fraternity Gang Rape 68–70
Freud, Sigmund 40, 85–7, 115, 127
Frodo 18, 77, 114
Fryer, Donald S. 43
Functionalism 84–5

George, St. 75
Gesar 109
Gnosticism 34–5
goths 26, 34

Hardy, Thomas 2
Hedges, Chris 130
Heller, Sophia 146
Herakles, Hercules 39, 72, 76, 109, 110–11, 113, 126
Herder, Johann Gottfried 89
Hesiod, on creation 7, 38, 39
  on Pandora 48
  on sacrifice 99
Hinduism 25, 43, 74, 117, 133–4

Hitler, Adolf 29–32, 127–8, 144
Homer 8, 43, 126, 134
Hopi 50–1
Huber, Peter 124–5
Huron 49–50
Hurston, Zora Neale 56–7

Iblis 32–3
Ignatius of Antioch 66
Iliad 9, 123, 126
initiation 26, 60, 62–70, 75, 85, 99
  of girls 104
  and shamanism 64
Isis 9, 37, 87, 104, 105–7
Islam 15, 31, 32–3, 101
  afterlife in 137–9
  and Axial Age 134
Ivan, Prince 114–16

Jainism 43, 116–18, 140
Jay, Nancy 103–4
Jerusalem 123–4
  in Islam 137
Jesus 71–2, 78, 79, 110, 116, 118
  and Axial Age 135
  and eschatology 132
  meaning for Ignatius of Antioch 66
  quest of the historical 83
Jivaro 102
Judaism 31, 101, 123
Jung, Carl Gustav 87–8, 115, 144, 146
Jünger, Ernst 119–20, 144, 146

Krappe, A. H. 8

Langer, Susanne 134
Leadbeater, C. W. 65–6
LeShan, Lawrence 129–30
Lévi-Strauss, Claude 36, 82, 85
Lewis, C. S. 5, 9, 18
Limba people, Sierra Leone 46–7, 96

Lincoln, Bruce 125
Loki 53, 55–6, 58–60, 97
Lord of the Rings 18, 77
Losev, Aleksei F. 80–1
Lovecraft, H. P. 34–5
Luria, Aleksandr R. 8–9

Maenads 51–2, 66
Mahavira 116–18
Malekula 136
Malemba 20–1
Malinowski, Bronislaw 84–5
Mandan 64
Manichaeism 44
Marduk 38, 75–6
 and war 122–3
Maya, myths of 6, 37
Mecca 15, 32
Merkur, Dan 86
Milton, John 31, 33–4, 53, 121, 145
Moses 71–2, 110, 118
myth, as story 3–4
 and bonding 26–7

Narnia 5, 9, 18
New Guinea 64–6, 124–5, 127
Nietzsche, Friedrich 43, 52
Number, The 67–8

Odin 55–6, 58, 66–7, 102
 see also Wotan
Odysseus 77, 91, 113–14, 135–7
Odyssey 9, 91, 136
Orestes 17–18
Orpheus 51–2, 110
Osiris 37, 106–7
Otto, Walter 52
Oz 74, 109, 114

Pandora 7, 48
Paradise Lost 31, 121, 145

Persephone 51, 106, 137
Plato 90–1, 134
Pollsmoor Prison 67–8
Pure Land Buddhism 140
Purusha 99–100

Rama, Ramayana 42, 72–4, 145
Re, Ra 37
Ricoeur, Paul 7, 16, 82
romanticism 88–90
Rougemont, Denis de 29–30

Sandy, Peggy 68–70
Satan 22–3, 29, 31, 40, 145
 and St. Michael 121–2
 as twin of God 43–5, 53–4
'Satanic Panic' 23–4
Schelling, Wilhelm von 80–9, 124
Segal, Robert 89
shaman, shamanism 19, 58, 89, 136
 initiation and 65–6, 104–6
Shiva 72, 74–5, 133–4
Sita 72–4
Snow White 77
sociopath 59–61
South Africa 67–8
Star Trek 45
Star Wars 9, 27, 86–7, 125
Steinberg, Jonny 67–8
Storm of Steel 119–20, 143
Susanoo 76, 97–8, 112

Ta'aroa 40–1
Tahiti 40–1
Tannen, Ricki Stefanie 58–9
terrorism 128–9
Thales 95–6
Theseus 76, 77
Thompson, Mark 58
Tiamat 38–9, 75–6, 122–3

Index

Titanic 1–3, 7, 27
Tolkien, J. R. R. 7, 18 *see also* Frodo, *Lord of the Rings*
trickster 35, 45, 53–61, 85, 96, 97, 142–3
Turtle Island 49–50

Vishnu 42–3

Wheeler, Brannon 15
witch hunts, European 22–3
witchcraft, meaning of 16, 22–3, 25–7, 85, 142

witches, African 20–1
 Russian 21–2
Wizard of Oz, The 74
Wotan 121–2, 126 *see also* Odin

Yakut 105
Yamato-takeru 111–13

Zen 104, 107–8
Zeus 17, 39, 48, 53, 72, 84, 110–11
Zoroastrianism 31, 44, 122
Zuni 54–5
Zurvanism 44

www.ingramcontent.com/pod-product-compliance
Lightning Source LLC
Chambersburg PA
CBHW060955230426
43665CB00015B/2211